STILL WATER FLY-FISHING

Plate I

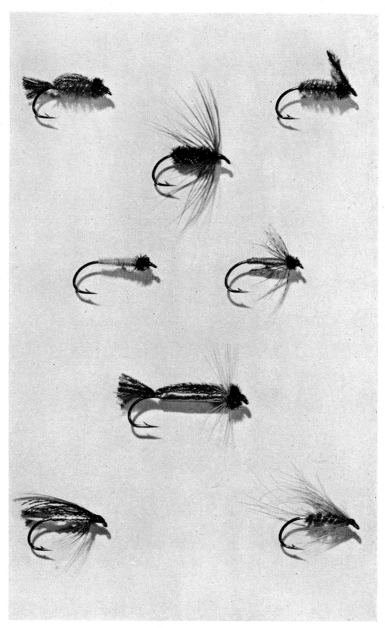

From left to right:
BROWN & GREEN NYMPH   BROWN NYMPH
BLACK & PEACOCK SPIDER
GREEN & YELLOW NYMPH   GREEN NYMPH
JERSEY HERD
ALEXANDRA   PRETTY-PRETTY

STILL WATER FLY-FISHING

A MODERN GUIDE TO ANGLING IN RESERVOIRS AND LAKES

By T. C. IVENS

DEREK VERSCHOYLE
THIRTEEN PARK PLACE, ST. JAMES'S
LONDON S.W.1

First Published in 1952 by
DEREK VERSCHOYLE LIMITED
THIRTEEN PARK PLACE, ST. JAMES'S
LONDON, S.W.1

Printed in Great Britain
by Spottiswoode, Ballantyne and Company Limited
London and Colchester

TO RUTH

who sends me fishing, and makes me glad to be home
again; and who also did the line drawings
for this book

ACKNOWLEDGMENTS

I WISH TO ACKNOWLEDGE my debt to the many people without whose help this book would have been less complete.

To Mr R. L. Marston, Editor of *The Fishing Gazette*, whose friendly criticism made the original articles out of which this book developed such a success; to Drs O.L. Meehean, W. Hagen and A.V. Tunison of the US Fish and Wildlife Service and to Mr E. D. le Cren of the Freshwater Biological Association, all of whom exchanged long informative letters with me; to Mr D.F. Leney, of Surrey Trout Farms and Mr K.B.S. Brown of Blagdon, whose information on hatchery work in England was most helpful, and to Dr T.T. Macan of the Freshwater Biological Association who read and criticized the chapter on stocking; to Messrs A. Smith and A.R. Kelly of the Pemberton-Warren Trout Acclimatization Society, who gave me much helpful information on their pioneer project in Western Australia; to Mr R.B. Finney of R.B. Finney Ltd. whose genius with a camera and enthusiasm in a new sphere of activity resulted in some very interesting photographs; to Mr J.E. May, the famous amateur caster, who gave me some very helpful information and checked the chapter on casting; to Mr Dick Walker with whom I have corresponded at length, and whose opinions I respect although I may not always agree with them; to Captain L. A. Parker who is always willing to pass on to others the information he has gained in a lifetime of angling; to the officers of the Mid-Northants Water Board who gave permission for photographs to be taken on their waters, to the Bristol Waterworks Company for permission to publish Mr C. E. White's photograph of their famous Blagdon Water; to the Town Clerk of Bridgewater who supplied the photograph of Durleigh Reservoir.

Lastly, and perhaps most importantly, my thanks are due to all those men whose company by the water has made my fishing so enjoyable.

PREFACE

IN 1951 MY SERIES OF ARTICLES entitled 'Reservoir Trout Fishing' was published in *The Fishing Gazette*. It is true that I had hoped one day to write a book on the subject, but most certainly I did not imagine that it would appear so soon. That it has done so is very largely owing to the many letters received expressing the wish that my articles should appear in book form.

This book is an expansion of these articles. The text has of course been amended, new chapters have been added and, perhaps what is most important, methods discussed in the original articles and which were shown by enquiring letters to have been inadequately treated have been re-explained in detail to make sure of complete clarity.

It is probably as little true to say that the methods outlined in this book are applicable to all still waters holding trout wherever they may be, as it would be to suggest that Skues' description of nymphing on a chalk stream could be applied also in every respect to the Teign, the Ure, or for that matter the Klamath. Because so many anglers have said in effect 'all still waters are the same', I have tried in Chapter 12 to explain just why this is not so. Shallow waters have never received adequate literary treatment, while the deep lakes have probably received more than their fair share. In spite of the wealth of literature on the lake-fishing of Bala, Tal-y-Llyn, Loch Lomond and Loch Leven, to mention but a few, little has been written of the technique of fishing from the bank rather than from a boat when visiting these waters. Most deep lakes whether they be modern reservoirs or the result of glacial action have at least some wadable, weeded shallows along their margins. Where there are weeds there will be fish and where there are fish, there should go the angler. Wherever marginal shallows occur, something of the new approach to be found in the following chapters can be applied.

I believe that in England and Wales a total of 50,000 fishermen fish still waters for trout; 25,000 of them will be still water specialists, men who go to the waterside on every available occasion. The inclusion of Scotland would double the numbers.

Not all of these men use the fly; many who prefer fly-fishing will in fact spin in still waters because they have found it difficult to take fish on fly.

It is understandable but nevertheless a pity, for when the diligence and study normally applied to river fly-fishing are given whole-heartedly to lake waters, these difficulties cease to be insurmountable and the fly can be shown to be as effective a method as any. I sincerely hope this book may persuade threadliners to give the fly another chance, basing their approach on the behaviour of fish in still water. The novice angler will find limited success with threadline in his earlier attempts, much more success and easier of attainment than he will with fly, but in the hands of a competent and studious angler the fly over a season will give as good results as the threadline minnow. There can be no doubting that the rhythm and beauty of fly casting are sources of delight and satisfaction in themselves, making mastery of the technique a soul-satisfying experience unknown to the threadline addict.

Just as Skues' writing of nymphing in rivers has contributed something of importance to my technique, so I hope those who fish rivers may find ideas of mine which could be adapted to river work.

Primarily this book is written about Midland reservoirs, but it will also apply in greater part to eutrophic[1] lakes containing trout anywhere in the world. If the trout are large, averaging 2lb or over, then my flies and methods will be found to be satisfactory. Where the fish average perhaps 1lb then the flies might well be two sizes smaller. Where lakes are of the oligotrophic[2] type, and bottom feed is restricted, fish will be relatively easier to take on fly and dry-fly may well from time to time give better results than wet-fly.

I am always glad to hear from anglers about their waters and I sincerely hope that anyone who has tried my methods will write to me of his successes and failures.

1. A word explained on Page 75.
2. A word explained on Page 75.

CONTENTS

ILLUSTRATIONS

Photographs

Diagrams

CHAPTER ONE

On the Choice of a Rod

ALTHOUGH IT IS TRUE that the man with but one rod loses no sleep or fishing-time deciding which rod he will take with him, Hobson's choice where rods are concerned is not an enviable situation. Although far from being particularly well off, I have always acted on the premise that one should not attempt to make a single rod serve widely differing purposes. Rather should one acquire several rods each suited to a different type of fly work.

I have met many men with a selection of rods at their disposal but, all too often, 50 per cent of each collection consists of rods of similar type. Never have I come across an angler with a rod specially designed for 'Reservoir Trouting'.

I believe our Midland reservoirs provide some of the finest fly-fishing in Britain: certainly, few rivers can produce fish which average so great a weight or such grand condition, and yet from the tackle point of view these reservoirs might be non-existent. Possibly this is due to the fact that there is no book dealing in detail with 'Blagdon-type' waters. Occasionally writers refer to Blagdon, but with the exception of Mr G. D. Luard they appear to have used boats. Mr Luard, I feel, half hit upon the basic truth of reservoir fishing, namely, that the well-equipped and skilled bank fisherman will usually take more fish than the boat fisherman.

Thus it has come about that the fishing public has not been educated to understand that river tackle is, in 95 per cent of cases, hopelessly unsuited for use on reservoirs. I am not going to bother my head, or yours, with gear for boat fishing; there are few tackle problems in this connection, for the boat angler can approach to within easy casting distance of his fish. Not so the bank fisherman: he requires a special skill which can be achieved only with specialized tackle.

The river fisherman with no experience of reservoirs may well wonder why specialized tackle is so necessary. I believe he will find the reasons as he reads on, for I have been at pains to give as accurate a picture of reservoir fishing as is possible on paper.

Many of the best reservoirs occupy shallow valleys, and water of only 6ft depth is often to be found as much as 100yd from the shore. Such marginal shallows with their extensive weed-beds are usually the best holding water on the reservoir. The angler must be able to cover as much of this 'belt' as possible. His problem, unlike that of the river angler, is not the avoiding of overhanging trees, near-by shrubs and so on, but the casting of as long a line as possible as often as he is able. He will not be bothered by the 'flora (or fauna) of the hinterland', for he will usually wade 10yd or more out from the margin, which is usually clear of vegetation. (Water-authorities usually take care to keep trees and rushes well above high-water mark to prevent decaying vegetation from fouling the bottom.) Thus the problem of casting a narrow loop does not present itself. Even fishing from the dams does not necessitate a narrow loop, you merely throw high at the back.

I have often seen powerfully-built, fit men on the water using 9ft 6in rods weighing about 6½oz. At the end of a day of long casting – that is, casting an average distance of 23yd to 25yd, they are all but collapsed with fatigue. It is so unnecessary – the collapse, not the long casting. In nearly every case you find that the man is the proud owner of a first-class rod by a first-class maker, but that his rod is nearly always tip-actioned and designed for throwing a short line with a narrow loop, on a river.

Tip-actions are the devil on a reservoir. My first rod was such an one: a delightful rod until I had 18yd of line in the air. At that point the upper part of the rod became overloaded.

By definition a tip-actioned rod is one whose bending is focused nearer to the top than to the butt. The upper part of the rod assumes a marked curve because it is not powerful enough to resist bending and thereby force the lower part of the rod to work. Long casting demands that the whole rod contribute to the effort, but many rods are so constructed that the top can be overloaded while the butt is idle. Since only part of the rod is working fully, only that part can release much energy. On the other hand a rod which works through its full length imparts a much greater impulse to the line and obviously is better suited to long casting. Again, once any part of a rod has reached its optimum, no increased effort on the part of the angler will effect noticeable increase in distance. So said Joannès Robin, author of *La Canne à Mouche à Truite, Objet d'Art*.

I am sure that by this time, some of my readers who use 'Balanced' or 'Torpedo-head' lines will be prepared to disagree with what I have written. To 'clear my yard-arm', let me say I am not concerned with 'balanced' lines, which present a completely different set of mechanical problems in casting. I use and strongly recommend double-tapered lines, for often the line will pass over a fish, and the heavy shadow of the torpedo-head is a sure fish-scarer. Likewise these lines often disturb the water both on delivery and pick-up.

No, the ideal rod must be capable of handling 22yd of line in the air, and be capable furthermore of initiating a forward impulse to the line great enough to allow up to 6yd more of line to be shot. In other words, we want a rod capable of casting 28yd of line and a longish cast (with single fly) on the end of it. Such a rod must have an all-through action and for preference should be butt-actioned. It is enough to say that the centre and top of the rod must be stiffish.

If only casting had to be considered in choosing the rod the natural choice would be one of those jewel-like rods which Messrs Hardy Bros so aptly name the 'Koh-i-noor'. But casting is not the whole of the story, and the powerful tournament rod falls down in several vital aspects.

The ideal rod must not be unduly stiff, for in high summer when long casting is perhaps most necessary it is sometimes essential to use small flies, or nymphs to fine gut (I believe one should try to avoid a cast as fine as 3x in water containing heavy fish. It is fairer angling to rise, hook and net few fish on 2x, than to rise, hook and lose many fish on 3x and finer points. Many of these 'pricked' or hooked fish become conditioned to be non-risers). The shortish, powerful tournament rod is too stiff to be safe, I feel, even when using 2x gut or its equivalent in nylon.

There is yet another reason why our rod should not be as rigid as a tournament rod. Often a fish has to be held hard, or slid over the top of a weed-bed, therefore resilience is required. Rigidity and resilience (ability to flex without fracture) militate against one another, as was recently stated by Robin in *La Pêche Indépendante* and indirectly by Dick Walker in his recent thesis on *Split Bamboo Constructions*.

A rigid rod would break sooner or later under the rough treatment mentioned, and even if it remained unfractured itself, would cause many breakages when 'holding' fish. As ever we are seeking the best compromise.

The necessary power and resilience will be found in an all-through-actioned (butt-biased) rod 10ft in length, weighing about 8½oz and consisting of two pieces. The cane should not be heat-treated to great hardness or the rod will be too stiff; on the other hand the cane must not be soft or the rod will be sloppy and worse than useless. The fittings should not be excessively light, for durability in the face of hard work is a first necessity.

It is extraordinary how many people are horrified at the idea of an 8½oz rod. Such a weapon is not the fisherman-killer many angling writers, particularly those on the other side of the Atlantic, would have you believe. My 'ideal rod' tires me far less casting a very long line than does the 6½oz tip-actioned rod, since the former works from tip to butt and handles the line with ease.

When casting with a butt-actioned rod one habitually 'follows through' after 'punching'; one does not attempt to 'stop' the action. This is possibly because the whole rod is moving and possesses high momentum of its own: it is physically impossible to 'stop' it at eleven o'clock as one can a light, tip-actioned rod. This 'follow through' or 'drift' is said to result in the wide loop associated with butt-actioned rods, but as you will read in Chapter 4, this probably is not the true cause. However, it is that 'follow through' that makes casting with butt-actioned rods far less tiring than casting and stopping a tip-actioned rod.

The 'ideal rod' must be kind to the fisherman, he must be reasonably fresh to make the most of the evening rise, though, truth to tell, however exciting the rise may be it never seems to produce the fish it appears to promise.

As we have said, reservoir fishing demands continuous long casting and great concentration. The less you have to rest, the longer your fly is in the water, and all other things being equal the length of time you are fishing will determine the size of your bag, over a period. Your ability to stand up to a day of 'The Contemplative Man's Recreation!' on a reservoir, will largely depend on the efficiency of the rod (and line) you are using for the job in hand.

I would not care to recommend any catalogued rod as ideal for this work – I do not know of one that has been designed for it. But in 1950 I took delivery of a rod made to my requirements by Messrs J. J. S. Walker, Bampton, and used the rod for the first time on 30 July of that year. Fishing a large shallow bay and casting across wind I soon got the 'feel' of the rod, and after some fifteen minutes turned to try casting up wind. Twenty yards of line went out effortlessly and to crown my satisfaction a fish hit the fly almost as it touched the water. Two and a half minutes later a trout of 3lb 7oz was on the bank. There and then the rod was christened 'The Iron Murderer'.

In 1951 there was only the one rod in existence, but in 1952 many more anglers were using similar rods. Some day I may improve on that rod, but at the moment it is, for me at any rate – the best reservoir rod of the many rods I have handled.

It is often suggested in angling journals that split cane has had its day. The alternatives at the moment are steel and glass fibre. My guess is that glass fibre is the more dangerous rival, but it must not be forgotten that the use of synthetic resins has given bamboo a new lease of life. Much has recently been learned about correct heat-treatment of bamboo. The old uncontrolled 'curing' and hardening will rapidly give way to the carefully worked-out heat treatment systems, evolved by such organizations as The Forest Products Laboratory of Madison, Wisconsin.

4

The greatest danger to the split cane rod lies in several faults of construction and design which appear to continue to exist merely because they always have existed.

We continue to fit ferrules which are so designed that there is a ·02in (approx) step down in the diameter of the stick immediately above the ferrule, and it is therefore not surprising that breaking off above the male ferrule is so common a failure. Again, although the node of the culm is recognized as a weak spot, we continue to group the nodal points of the strips in threes instead of spiralling them and thereby avoiding more than one node at a given point along the stick. The delightful varnish finish of the high-grade English rod is world famous, but it nevertheless causes flash, and eventually it cracks and the rod has to be cleaned off, retied and varnished. Surely any protection needed could be impregnated into the skin of the cane. Rod-tyings today are quite superfluous, the present urea formaldehyde or resorcinal resin glues are waterproof and there is no danger of the bonded strips parting company. But the greatest and most easily cured fault lies in the use of agate rings. It is quite impossible to avoid the occasional cracked ring when travelling, and into the bargain the agate substitute rings – particularly the transparent ones – groove. All these lined rings are expensive and could well be replaced by the highly efficient rust-proof and unbreakable steel alloy rings used on many high-grade rods in USA and also on the English 'Apollo' rods.

As to the intermediate rings, it is a case of 'you pays your money and you takes your choice!' It has been claimed that snake rings give little line friction when shooting, but I nevertheless like a bridge-ring. All intermediates should be heavily chromed to resist wear and should be reasonably large to facilitate shooting.

This list of shortcomings of the English rod must make some readers feel like asking why on earth I use them. The plain fact is that deficient in some respects as they are, they are still the most beautiful tools for their price produced anywhere in the world. While a first-class rod in England can be bought for as little as £12, its counterpart in America would cost much more. It must not be thought that the American-built rod is the acme of perfection. American ferrules are not so robustly constructed and well finished as ours, and their rods as a whole would disappoint most English fishermen who so often judge a rod on appearance. But in case we start to feel too superior we should remind ourselves that while we have merely maintained the standard of our 1935 rods, the Americans have been going ahead and today some of their better builders could probably teach us a great deal, particularly with regard to rod tapers.

The American angler is tackle-conscious – perhaps too much so – and his tackle industry is quick to put new technology to practical use.

The result has been some very weird pieces of equipment of truly amazing variety, but nevertheless our casting records have travelled westward.

The 'Casting Tournament' has long been regarded in England as a sporting event in which 'freak tackle' is made to do things which would scare any fish clean out of the water. Nevertheless it must be admitted that the rules are equal for all, and the 4oz rod with the greatest power-weight ratio is likely, when used with a suitable line, to put up the best performance. There is little doubt that tournament casting has done much to improve all tackle. In recent years, however, there has been a marked swing away from purely tournament gear towards competition casting with normal fishing tackle. 'Skish' as the new competitive casting is named, is organized in USA on national lines, clubs competing in divisions much as do our football clubs.

The formation of these clubs has considerably widened the choice of casters for international tournament work, since the man who promises to shape well gets the necessary practice and coaching.

Here, few men would consider going to a professional for tuition in casting. Most are content to spend an hour or two with a friend and then muddle along by the waterside as best they can. I speak from experience, for I too muddled along in the same way. Chance brought me into contact with a really good amateur caster, Phil Lupton of Harrogate. We visited his casting pool, and within half an hour he had ironed out a faulty stance and diagnosed several other faults. A month later I was casting 5yd farther than I had ever cast before, and with exactly the same tackle.

Since my series of articles in *Fishing Gazette* first appeared, several readers have expressed polite disbelief as to the distances I have claimed to cast. It has been noticeable that none of them is a reservoir specialist. There is little doubt that today the best potential tournament distance-casters are to be found amongst the reservoir anglers. Certainly the average river fisherman can rely upon good tuition and good example of style from many of the men he will meet on a reservoir. Given such contacts and the necessary specialized equipment, there is little doubt that the novice reservoir angler will add 10yd to his cast in a season in the 'Reservoir School of Casting'.

CHAPTER TWO

Tackle and Equipment

THE ROD IS BUT ONE SPECIALIZED ITEM of tackle for use on a reservoir. The remainder of the equipment is no less important, and I propose in this chapter to deal with every other essential item with the exception of casts and flies which are dealt with separately.

The rod can never perform well unless the line is suited to it. In tournament casting, the enthusiast experiments with torpedo-heads of varying lengths and tapers (and consequently of varying weights) until he finds the line which gives him his best performance. Just as our rod was a compromise, so must be the line. I admit that a torpedo-head line almost casts itself: 15yd of line in the air, moving fast, will enable 10yd or 12yd of line to be shot from the hand. It does not require a long rod to do the job: an 8-footer will do it, provided it is stiff enough to develop high tip-speed. But as I said before, these lines are bad under actual fishing conditions owing to the large diameter of the head causing heavy shadows on the bottom, and surface-splash, too, on occasion. The ordinary double-tapered line is our best compromise, and the rod I described will require size No3. The rod will just about handle a No4 line, but again size 4 brings the diameter up. I strongly advise that whenever you find your rod requires a line intermediate between two sizes, you choose the lighter line. Such a line which leaves the rod slightly under-loaded, will cast as far as the heavier line which would overload the rod. The light line, however, has the ultimate advantage since it adds years to the life of your rod, and enables you to pick up a very much longer line from the water. This last is an extremely important point when picking up to throw to a fish which has just risen, an occasion when speed is all important.

I think it is worth while to mention that when a maker recommends a No3 or No4 line to balance the action of a rod, he is thinking in terms of river fishing, that is to say, he is reckoning that on the average the angler will false cast 12yd or so of line, and shoot another three. We have stated that we may have as much as 22yd of line in the air, and such a length approximately doubles the load on the tip of the rod, since the extra 10yd is a length of heavy level line. Again that increased load must be given higher initial speed in order that the very much longer line may straighten before dropping. I therefore suggest that if you wish to use a tip-actioned rod for long casting you use a line a size lighter than is customary. You will find that the lighter line, because of its higher ratio of 'diameter to weight per unit-length', has greater air resistance and will cast only as far as the heavier line, but you will not strain or break the rod in casting or picking up a long line. Perhaps I seem unduly concerned about the safety of the rod. 'Light tournament rods cast these heavy lines and pick them up,' you say. Yes, they do! But they are not doing it for hour after hour, day after day. Please accept my assurance, reservoir fishing can, and frequently does, break rods.

Modern fly-lines vary enormously in their finish and it is most necessary that I make some comment which may help the novice to avoid a wrong choice.

Many lines are far too highly polished – a sure indication of a hard finish which will crack. In no branch of fly-fishing is a smooth, supple dressing so desirable. The line is subjected to very severe treatment in constant long casting and shooting and, in addition, is bunched in the hand when recovering line to work the fly. I have used 'Kingfisher' lines for years and have found them excellent. The quality of the dressing and silk leaves nothing to be desired, while at the same time they are one of the cheapest lines on the market. It is only fair to add that several anglers have reported to me the excellence of Messrs Farlow's lines. I can make no comment of my own as I have not used them, but I can say that they have the same supple finish as 'Kingfisher' lines and are similarly priced.

Nylon lines are lighter per diameter than silk lines, and, having greater wind resistance, are not suited to long casting. In addition their lightness makes them very unsuitable for casting in or into a wind no matter what the length of line may be. As we shall mention in a later chapter, casting into a wind is sometimes the means of picking up a lot of fish.

A few days ago, I met a river fisherman who was most enthusiastic about nylon fly lines.

'No bother at all,' he said, 'I wind in my line when I pack up and there it stays until I want it again.'

Quite apart from the lazy attitude which is fatal to good fishing, our friend had entirely ignored the fact that one removes and dries a fly line more to safeguard the dressing than the silk. I cannot over-emphasize the importance of getting the line off the reel as soon as you get home after fishing. Make a point of doing it before you eat – I do: that way it is not forgotten.

During the close season my lines remain hanging in loose coils from pegs in a wardrobe. Outside-workshops do not provide a suitable atmosphere for lines. Long periods of low temperatures are followed by muggy periods when walls stream with water. Such extremes of

Plate II

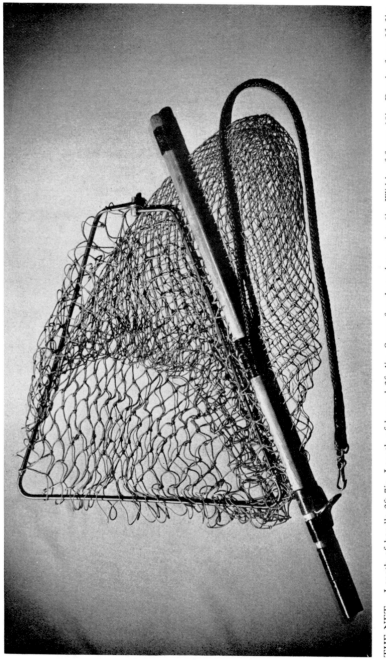

THE NET. Length of handle 2ft 7in. Length of lanyard 3ft 4in. Screw ferrule to brass ring 6in. Width of frame 18in. Depth of net 2ft 3in. Handle is marked off as a measuring stick.

Plate III

POSITION 1. Net slung; cannot interfere with casting or comfort.

Plate IV

POSITION 2. Net pulled to side; clip unfastened

Plate V

POSITION 3. Net resting on the bottom, leaving both hands free to handle rod and reel, but ready for instant use. Time from Position 1 to Position 3: 4 seconds.

temperature and humidity are bad for lines. Bedrooms provide the most suitable storage conditions in most homes – and you can state this authoritatively to your own household.

Just before opening day I wipe down my lines with a soft cloth *lightly* sprinkled with pure turpentine. This cleans off any dust and old grease and leaves the line in clean condition ready for a thorough rubbing down with 'Cerolene'.

And now to the reel.

With an 8½oz rod you may safely use an 8oz reel. We are advised in many publications to use a reel which balances the rod on a fulcrum about 3in above the grip. This is over-simplification of the problem. The reel ought to balance the rod in movement, and with our butt-actioned rod you will find that any reel between 6oz and 9oz appears to balance the action. I have not bothered to think out the reason for this yet, but tip-actioned rods are by no means as tolerant of deviation in reel-weight. However, this is only of theoretical interest, since you will only obtain the necessary line capacity with reels of 7½oz upwards. As a river fisherman you probably feel safe with 30yd of double-tapered line and 20yd of backing. As a reservoir fisherman, I used to feel safe with 30yd of double-tapered line and 60yd of backing. As a result of one or two near tragedies, I now hope I am safe with a 30yd double-tapered line and 100yd of backing.

On a river the banks set a limit to the distance a trout can run. That is true of a reservoir, too, but in this case the other bank may be 800yd away, and you cannot follow a fish out to the middle.

My first large reservoir trout, a fish of 5lb 3oz, took me down to my last 10yd of line when I was using a total of 90yd. A week later exactly, after I had gone over to the 130yd line, a fish took out well over 100yd of line in each of the two long runs he made before the hook tore free. (I shall have something to say on small hooks in Chapter 5.) Two years later, a foul-hooked fish of only 1lb 7oz stripped about 80yd of line off before I stopped him: he was hooked just near the vent and netting him was a pantomime. Every time I brought him to the net, tail first and head down, so he was off again. These experiences are not unusual. A friend using 90yd of line was broken when a fish took him down to the drum last year. You see, the fish are cruisers by habit: they do not dive for a hole under the bank or for the shelter of a rock as does the river fish. Having no home, so to speak, they often head out into the lake and keep going. A fish hooked in shallows usually makes a very long, fast run for deeper waters, and as we have said these reservoirs have wide, shallow margins and the fish has some way to go. When fishing in the deep water off the dams the fight is one of depth rather than distance, but now and then up comes the exception that tests the rule. On 18 May 1952 while fishing a

'Jersey Herd' from the dam, a fish hit me and immediately made a fast surface-run over the horizon. I had visions of a 'tenpounder' which were not shattered until I saw the fish fifteen minutes later – foul-hooked in the tail. When I netted him some ten minutes later the hook dropped free. He pulled the balance down to 3lb 10oz.

I hope what I have said will have made it clear that you must have at least 100yd of line, and the reel should be of large diameter to facilitate line recovery. I use, and again recommend, the Hardy 'St George' reel. This reel of 3¾in diameter carries with ease 30yd of No3 line and 100yd of 18lb breaking-strain flax backing. Whatever the reel, do not cram line on to the drum. When you are playing a fish you often wind the line unevenly on to the drum, and a reel which was full becomes overfilled on one side. The backing line should be wound on tightly to prevent the casting line cutting down into it, a fruitful source of 'jams' when playing a fish. Have nothing to do with automatic fly reels. For the most part they are very heavy, and have small line-capacity. From time to time we read that the left-hand-wind fly reel is much to be preferred to the usual right-hand-wind reel. The writers emphasize the dangers of changing the rod to the left hand in those dangerous moments immediately following the 'take'. This criticism of right-hand-wind reels does not apply to lake fishing for no matter which hand you wind with, one hand must hold the rod while the other will hold recovered line. It is physically impossible to change the rod hand until the fish has run out the line held in the hand and by that time there is no danger in passing the rod to the left hand.

If wading is permitted then it must be regarded as essential. If, like me, you are blessed with big feet, then you have an advantage, in that your ordinary full thigh waders are long in the leg, and enable you to wade well out without resorting to trouser waders. If you are short in the leg then you will find trouser waders an advantage, though they are horrifying things if you have to make the very long walk round to the opposite bank. Rubber thigh waders with metal-studded soles are unnecessary, for you will be wading on sand or mud bottoms in the waters we are dealing with. When fishing from the stones of the dams, which become dreadfully slippery after a shower, you would be well advised to slip off your waders and put on a pair of plimsolls or, better still, rope-soled shoes, for these will permit you to swim for it. I once spent a nerve-racking hour and a half with an elderly man fishing from a steep dam with a hedge at the top. I packed up fishing and spent my time getting his fly out of the hedge, rather than have to fetch him out of the water when he attempted to scramble up and down the stones. Needless to say, he saw no risk and wrongly thought I was activated by altruistic motive only.

10

I always carry a small repair outfit and would like to pass on a method of patching rubber waders which I have found very good.

Patches on waders tend to lift, but this can be prevented by first patching with very thin crêpe rubber and then patching over the crêpe with Dunlop repair-sheet rubber. The crêpe alone will not stand up to wear.

Deep wading is cold work, and in the early spring I always wear two pairs of stockings, and use waders one size larger than my shoes. Loose waders are much warmer than a snug-fitting pair.

The wicker creel is not suitable for reservoir fishing if the fish average – as ours do – over $2\frac{1}{4}$lb. I use a strong, large, canvas haversack with two compartments. During the day if the weather is cool, I put my fish in a small pillow-case and leave them on the bank, for the weight of two or three fish would restrict my movements when casting. In hot weather, I like to hang fish up, out of the sun – the skin dries and the fish keep in better condition. I appreciate the wide strap of my haversack when carrying home the spoils.

And now the net.

The standard size throw-up net is a snare and delusion. I use a net of my own design, consisting of an 18in steel frame, triangular in shape, screwed into a handle 2ft 7in long. It is secured by a cord loop over my head. When a fish is hooked and all is well, the dog-leash clip is unhitched with the left hand, and the net front is rested on the bottom with the handle against my tummy for instant use. The net is very deep and needs to be, for quite often you deal with fish over 4lb in weight and we know 8lb fish are there. The net interferes in no way when fishing, as you will see from the photographs. And how wonderful it is to have a net large enough to make a clean job of netting a heavy fish at the first attempt! I suppose I am asking for trouble, but it is, nevertheless, true at the moment to state that I have never lost a fish at the net when using this type of net, and last year it secured a $6\frac{1}{4}$lb grilse with the same ease.

If the equipment we have mentioned seems over-much for an occasional outing on a reservoir, may I mention that the outfit is grand for sea-trouting, although I found the rod a trifle powerful for these soft-mouthed fish. The butt-actioned rod will switch-cast very nicely, which makes it useful on a river.

CHAPTER THREE

....

Nylon and the Reservoir Fisherman

'SOME SWEAR BY IT; while others swear at it.' Those words fairly sum up the nylon controversy.

The substance has suffered as much at the hands of those who laud its qualities as from those who loathe everything about it, including its name. When we first used it we were all in the dark, but we soon found that knots such as the 'Figure-of-Eight' and 'Taverner's Loop', which were reliable in gut, were anything but reliable in nylon. We experimented, and before long, having found a knot which was less useless than the others, we were writing letters to angling journals to let our colleagues into the secret. The result was a multiplicity of knots of varying value, whose only recommendations were those of their proud inventors. Most of us tried them all; we learned to tie none of them correctly before passing on to the next, and having gone through the lot more or less unsuccessfully, we pronounced nylon as being 'more interesting than tough'.

Doctor Barnes, Captain Parker and others, changed the story by carrying out machine-tests in which results were directly comparable, and we now have the basic three knots, the 'Blood-Bight-Loop', the 'Three Turn Blood', and the 'Tucked-Half-Blood'. The result of the discovery of these knots was that more anglers began to use nylon. At this point we came up against a second set of problems connected with breakage of the strand for which there was no apparent reason.

Nylon, of course, has little strength when first extruded like spaghetti through a hole in a steel plate. The chain-molecule of nylon is very long, 1,000 atoms or more, and the substance achieves its high tensile strength when these long molecules are forced to lie parallel to one another when the relatively soft, worm-like, extruded form of nylon is drawn out by stretching, while running over a system of rollers revolving at different speeds. Before this stretching, the molecules lie higgledy-piggledy; after stretching, their ends have been drawn in, and the monofilament exerts its greatest resistance to those stresses which operate parallel to its axis. Drawn metallic tubing gains its tensile strength from a similar molecular rearrangement. If analogy is possible, we may liken our nylon molecules to wool fibres. Worsted yarns have their fibres parallel to the axis and fine yarns are comparatively strong. Woollen yarns on the other hand show no such neat arrangement of the fibres, and diameter for diameter are weaker than worsted yarns.

When, however, these drawn substances are subjected to vibration, and forces are exerted at right angles to the axis of the drawn substance, the orientation of the molecules is broken down, and they again slowly assume their old unordered arrangement, and the tensile strength is markedly reduced. A breakage can then occcur without any great load being applied. In the case of metals this weakening is known as fatigue. I think we must accept it that nylon suffers from a very similar malaise.

Perhaps at this point it would be as well to recall the effect of nylon passing over a pick-up finger. During a recent holiday I used a Mitchell reel and German nylon to spin for sea-trout. The line initially broke at an evenly applied load of $6\frac{3}{4}$lb, but after only two hours' use the dry breaking load had been reduced to $4\frac{1}{4}$lb. Whether or not this experience is shared by others I do not know. I will only say that I did not experience anything like so great a loss of strength when using a length of this nylon as a fly cast. By a process of elimination I concluded that it was the bending over the pick-up finger which had engendered this weakness which extended over the whole length of used line. Needless to say, the weak and the good portions of the line appeared exactly similar. I am afraid I did not continue the experiment to find out whether $4\frac{1}{4}$lb was the lower limit of deterioration: I broke off the used portion and carried on spinning until an hour later, when conditions appeared right for the fly.

We all know about this peculiarity in nylon's behaviour, and it is not difficult to prevent trouble if we ignore the evidence of our eyes and throw away after reasonable use what appears to be a perfectly good cast or line.

But even now, when these peculiarities of nylon are accepted and allowed for, there still remains a drawback for the fly-fisherman, which results directly from one of the great attributes of nylon, namely: that the monofilament is available in continuous lengths of up to 110yd.

So often, I hear the complaint that nylon will not cast into a wind, that it lands in a 'bird's nest', or that it lags behind the line when long casting. Usually if I know the angler well enough to ask him questions or make suggestions, I find that he uses a nylon cast consisting either of a 3yd continuous length of monofilament, or a tapered nylon cast bought from his tackle dealer.

I am afraid, at times, that I 'kick' the tackle-maker rather hard, but in many cases criticism of his products is justified. All too often, unfortunately, the maker himself is not a first-class angler, and being but an average performer in his branch of fishing, never finds out the errors of design in his products. Let me digress to illustrate this point.

An angler has two fly rods, in his early days his long cast will be no more than 18yd, and at that distance all his gear can appear quite satisfactory. While his capability as a caster remains '18yd with the wind' he is most unlikely to discover that, while one set of tackle is suitable for casting up to 22yd, the other is quite capable of giving him 26yd. In fact I would go further: it *could* happen that because the long-casting outfit never has its power developed, the angler could believe that the less desirable rod, which was being forced to work at 18yd, was in fact much the better outfit. It is, I agree, more likely that at 18yd the better rod would be showing its worth, but please see my point: it would only be showing its worth to a man who really appreciated how a 26yd rod should behave. Again, the difference in design of two outfits, one of which has a 22yd capacity and the other a 26yd capacity is unbelievable: Ted Trueblood writing in *Field and Stream* about two years ago claimed that he had achieved a 20yd cast using a broomstick as a rod. It is the addition of distance beyond 22yd in which tackle design becomes important, and the perfection of tackle for long casting is essentially a job for a man who can get and has to get distance in his fishing.

I am going to concern myself with an item of equipment seldom referred to when casting problems are discussed, that is to say, the cast.

Double-tapered Nylon Casts

Reservoir trout fishing in the Midlands demands very long casting, and more often than not one has to cast across or up wind. Money spent on a most perfectly balanced rod and line of a 26yd or more potential, is money wasted unless the design of the cast for use with the outfit is of a similarly high order.

I soon found that I could not get my nylon cast to lie out straight when long casting. I was using three 40in lengths of nylon, tapering my casts from ·014in to ·010in. The material itself is less springy than gut and has not the same tendency to straighten of its own accord. In addition, I found in my reading that nylon has a lower specific gravity than that of gut, and immediately tumbled to the source of the trouble: for any given diameter and speed the momentum of gut will always be higher than that of nylon (this is also true of braided silk and nylon lines). In other words, nylon was too light to overcome wind resistance.

When long casting is required, the cast must carry its own weight and not rely upon being carried by the line. With normally tapered nylon casts, the line leads the cast all the way and the cast has not sufficient momentum to straighten itself in front of the line in the period when the line itself is coming to rest.

The problem seemed insurmountable, and I shelved it and went back to gut. But in November 1949, Al McClane, the Fishing Editor of *Field and Stream*, published details of nylon monofilament casts which are designed for speed casting without delivering the fly like a ton of bricks. (We can all get a light cast to straighten by lifting the rod point, or by pulling on the line at the last moment, but the hole the fly knocks in the water is a revelation to say the least of it.)

I chose two 'McClane Tapers' which suited my purpose and gave them a really good try out in 1950. During that season I used gut casts and nylon casts about equally. So good did I find these tapers, that in 1951 I completely gave up the use of gut and have every reason to be glad that I did so, for in high wind when both the ordinary gut and nylon casts were useless, these tapers performed with complete efficiency.

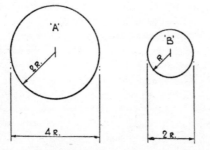

Diagram 1   CROSS SECTIONS OF 2 CASTS

The area of cross section 'A' is $\pi 4r^2$ and the diameter to be pushed through the air is 4r. Circle 'B' has a cross sectional area of πr^2 and a diameter of 2r. From this we see that for equal lengths of line, that with diameter 4r will be four times as heavy as that with diameter 2r. In other words, when we double the diameter we multiply the momentum at a given speed by four, the ratio of wind resistance to weight decreases, and the cast will travel farther before coming to rest. This greatly increased weight with slightly increased diameter is also the reason why thick fly-lines do not float so well as finer ones. Yet another advantage for the double-tapered line.

This was McClane's approach to the problem: he gained momentum and overcame wind resistance by using much thicker lengths of nylon in his casts, and at the same time he redistributed the weight and, in fact, evolved the 'Double-Tapered Cast'.

I give in the table below those of McClane's tapers which are most useful in reservoir fishing, followed by three tapers of my own (C, D and E) which meet the need for a really long 'leader' when fishing in conditions of bright sunlight. These very long leaders were developed to test Hewitt's theory, that it was better in bright conditions to lengthen the leader than to reduce the size of the point. Certainly appreciable lengthening of the leader appears to give as good results as a finer point, without any of the risks.

(I deliberately use the word 'leader', which the Americans use to describe the gut or nylon at the end of the line, so as to avoid the reader's confusing this piece of equipment with the actual throwing or casting of the fly.)

A) 40in of ·018in; 36in of ·017in; 7in of ·016in; 7in of ·014in; 7in of ·013in; 7in of ·012in; 28in of ·010in; length 11ft. General purposes.

B) 26in of ·020in; 24in of ·018in; 22in of ·016in; 18in of ·014in; length 7ft 6in. Heavy flies in strong cross or adverse winds.

C) 12in of ·016in; 12in of ·018in; 16in of ·020in; 12in of ·018in; 12in of ·016in; 12in of ·014in; 12in of ·012in; 12in of ·011in; 15in of ·010in; length 9ft 7in. This is a variation of a taper which Mc-Clane took down to ·008in, a little too light for work where fish are heavy. This is a grand taper for use under normally windy conditions and will allow of good casting up-wind. This leader will serve the novice-caster much better than the longer 'D' and 'E' tapers below.

D) 18in of ·016in; 18in of ·018in; 30in of ·020in; 14in of ·018in; 14in of ·016in; 10in of ·015in; 10in of ·014in; 10in of ·013in; 10in of ·012in; 12in of ·011in; 22in of ·010in; length 14ft. This leader is not easy to handle, but I have found that any awkwardness there may be is compensated for by the fact that fewer fish are put down in bright weather. The cast is also useful for fishing a nymph deep down.

E) 12in of ·016in; 12in of ·018in; 20in of ·020in; 12in of ·018in; 12in of ·016in; 12in of ·015in; 12in of ·014in; 12in of ·013in; 12in of ·012in; 20in of ·010in; Length 11ft 4in. This is my usual leader in light wind, and under sunny conditions.

There are endless variations of these tapers possible, and the reader must experiment until he finds a balance which suits his own rod and line. I feel that type D would be improved by using an even heavier nylon in the belly, and shall probably experiment along those lines as soon as I can obtain a suitably heavier monofilament. These casts are now marketed by Messrs J. J. S. Walker, Bampton of Alnwick.

Many readers of my articles in *Fishing Gazette* have written to ask me whether I would use nylon for all purposes. The answer is, that I would use nylon whenever I was not required to use a point finer than ·009in. In smaller sizes I have found that gut is stronger and infinitely more reliable than either English or French monofilament. Hardy's gut casts in these sizes are unbeatable.

Of the nylons available I prefer French. I had some unfortunate experiences with English nylon in early days, and also, later, with American nylon. French nylon is more reliable: I use 'Bell' brand and have great success with it. Last season I had fewer breakages than ever before: about 50 per cent of those I would have had using gut. My friends using 'Luxor', 'Racine Tortue', and so on, report similarly of their reliability. German nylons such as 'Platil' and 'Perlyl' are more flexible, and I do not use them for building fly-casts if I can avoid doing so, although diameter for diameter they are stronger than French nylons. 'Perlyl' suffers to my mind from having a shiny surface which must tend to flash more than the grey, matt-surfaced, French nylons.

There has been much comment recently on the relative visibility or invisibility of various dyes used for staining nylon. It is said that a certain shade of purple renders the casts less visible. It may be so, but it is seldom that the fish will be concerned with the reflected colour of the cast. More often than not in fly-fishing, the cast will be seen in silhouette, when, no matter what its colour, it will appear as a dark line against the lighted 'window'. Again, Hewitt's photographs show that objects lying in the surface cause depressions in the surface 'skin' through which light passes, to appear on the bottom as light-spots. What dye can overcome this defect?

I like my casts to be non-reflecting, and a neutral grey colour. Like a cinema-curtain, they will emit whatever colour of light is shone upon them, in other words the grey nylon will tend to become the greens and browns of weed and bottom. It is hard to conceive of any nylon being invisible in water unless it has a non-reflecting surface, has the same refractive index as water, and is as transparent as the water itself. I shall however make a prolonged and exhaustive test of violet-stained nylon in the coming year.

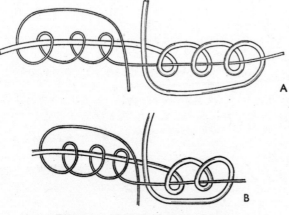

Diagram 2   THE BLOOD KNOT

The making of casts is a simple matter, but is so often bungled! The 'Blood' knot A is by far the best of knots for joining two strands, but I find in larger sizes that it pays to take two turns with the heavier strand and three with the lighter as in B. By this means the knot is drawn up evenly, and is stronger than the unevenly tightened knot which results from using three turns on both sides. The point is, that the lighter strand is more easily bent and tends to tighten before the heavy one.

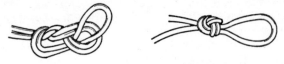

Diagram 3 THE BLOOD-BIGHT-LOOP

The 'Blood-Bight-Loop' is simple to make and is the only reliable loop-knot for nylon. It is important to note that it has one more *half*-turn than a 'Figure-of-Eight' knot. Care must be taken to draw up all strands evenly. I place the loop over a round nail and pull on both the long and short ends.

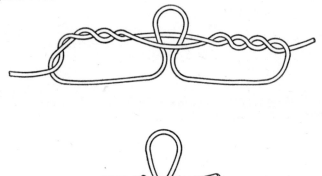

Diagram 4 THE BLOOD-LOOP DROPPER KNOT

I use this knot on the few occasions when I fish a dropper, the dropper length being attached to the loop by the 'Tucked-Half-Blood'.

Diagram 5 THE TUCKED-HALF-BLOOD

18

This knot is unbeatable. It first came to my notice in a list of knots given in *Field and Stream*, and was stated to have a breaking-strain of 98 per cent of that of the unknotted monofilament. I tied eighty specimens and tested them against other hitches used for the same purpose. In forty such tests against other knots, only twice was this knot beaten. The knots which beat the 'Tucked-Half-Blood' could not repeat their victory, which must therefore be attributed to bad tying of the 'Tucked-Half-Blood'. A further forty tests against a spring balance gave four breakages in the strand, and an average breaking percentage of 93 per cent, with two freak breakages of 50 per cent and 58 per cent not included in the average. Apart from these two freaks the lowest result was 84 per cent. It is important to pass the nylon through the eye from behind as shown in the diagram.

Since a 'Blood' knot gives an average breaking strain of about 85 per cent, it will often be found that when the fly is attached by means of the 'Tucked-Half-Blood' the point is lost when a break occurs, but this is more than compensated for by the fact that breakages occur much less frequently.[1]

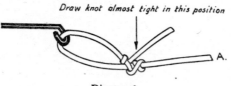

Draw knot almost tight in this position

A.

Diagram 6

It is usual to draw up the knot in front of the eye, as shown above, and then slide the knot down to the eye by pulling on the standing part A while holding the hook.

It is customary over here to pass the nylon through the eye of the fly, and knot onto the shank of the hook in front of the head of the fly. It is alleged that this gives the fly a clean entry into the water and keeps the hook shank in line with the cast.

I believe that this is of more importance in theory than in practice, and the Americans are by no means so insistent on the use of knots like the 'Double-Turle'.

We are all familiar with the fact that gut 'necks' seriously at the point where it passes through the ring of the fly, due to the hinging effect on the gut as the fly turns over when the line straightens in front

1. Very recently I have attached droppers by means of the 'Tucked-Half-Blood', passing the dropper nylon round the cast above a 'Blood' knot. It makes a tidy job, and at the moment of writing I have had no mishaps. There is a tendency, however, for the cast to be hinged by the weight of the dropper, necessitating occasional retying of the cast 'Blood' knot.

of or behind the caster. By knotting the cast to the eye itself this defect is entirely overcome, because the knot slips on the ring, and the cast, therefore, does not bend. Furthermore, when a fish is hooked it matters not from what direction the pull comes on to the fish; there is no bending of the gut or nylon with consequent weakening of the cast, for the knot slips round the ring as the direction of pull alters. I have not found in practice that the fly works any the less well for being attached to the cast in this way, but I did find when I first used this knot that the number of my breakages was reduced, a most important consideration.

Dotted lines show how knot slides round
eye and obviates 'Necking'

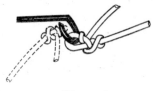

Diagram 7

Knotting is an art which is best divided into two separate parts: first the making of the turns, and secondly the forming of the finished knot. All anglers complete the first part more or less successfully, but few take trouble over the second and far more important part of the process.

Try this experiment. Make your turns for a 'Blood-Bight-Loop'; hold the loop and the two ends, and draw tight. Now have a close look at your knot. It is an even chance that you will find that strands which should lie parallel are, in fact, crossing over one another, and have not tightened evenly. This sort of thing can occur with any knot, and is best avoided by tightening evenly and slowly on the standing part or parts, at the same time drawing up the two ends. Great care must be taken to avoid overtightening, with consequent weakening of the monofilament in the knot itself. Nylon should always be tied dry.

It is a fact that your first twenty tyings of a new knot will have a lower average breaking strain than, say, the average BS of Nos 200 to 220. From this it follows that it pays to stick to a good knot when you find one, and avoid switching from knot to knot.

French and English Measurements

It is sometimes necessary to convert metric sizes to Anglo-Saxon sizes, and for the benefit of those who wish to construct tapers to the specifications given above, I give below a table for comparison purposes. The size-number of Continental nylons is the diameter expressed as hundredths of a millimetre. $1/100\text{mm} = \cdot0003937\text{in}$; therefore, to obtain the equivalent size in inches, we multiply the Continental size by $\cdot0003937$. Thus $26/100\text{mm}$ 'Bell' nylon is : $26 \times \cdot0003937\text{in}$ in diameter, ie $\cdot0102\text{in}$ or 1x.

Size in inches	Size in millimetres
·008	22/100 approx
·009	24/100 ,,
·010	26/100 ,,
·011	28/100 ,,
·012	30/100 ,,
·013	32/100 ,,
·014	35/100 ,,
·015	38/100 ,,
·016	40/100 ,,
·017	
·018	45/100 ,,
·019	
·020	50/100 ,,

It is impossible to find exact metric equivalents for any size in Anglo-Saxon measurements, and in several of the larger sizes of nylon monofil no near metric equivalents are available.

CHAPTER FOUR

....

Reaching Out for Distance

TO REFER IN CONVERSATION with another fly-fisherman to continous casting of distances greater than 23yd is to court disbelief. Very few fly men can throw a fly so far, and then only when the wind happens to be just right and their timing is a little better than usual. And yet it is not untrue to say that the experienced reservoir fisherman thinks of 23yd as commonplace.

'Debunking' is always amusing for a writer, and whenever it can do good it is well justified. In a discourse on casting one cannot help but debunk the generally accepted methods.

How often do we read of the 'book under the elbow' method of tuition, and how seldom does the counsellor refer to the necessity for keeping the line between the left hand and butt-ring tight!

Let us examine what happens when the average caster is at work. He grips the line with his left thumb and fore-finger and raises his rod to throw the line to the rear. The distance from his stationary left hand to the butt-ring increases as the rod lifts. After pausing briefly to allow his line almost to straighten at the rear, he punches the rod forward, and in so doing he decreases the distance between his left hand and the butt-ring. In other words, when he should be exerting a forward impulse against a tight line so as to gain maximum forward line speed, he is in fact punching against slack line, just as he would be were he to shoot line from his left hand as he made his forward punch.

The first step in improving your distance is to learn to follow the rod movements with the left hand so as to keep taut the line between the left hand and the butt-ring. If in the past you have neglected to do this, you will be amazed at the difference in distance this small left hand movement will make.

The tournament caster makes even greater use of his left hand, for he not only keeps his line tight as he punches, but also pulls on the line in time with his rod movements to accelerate the speed of his line. Earl Osten, the American caster, says that this style of casting developed on the west coast of America and was introduced into tournament casting by Marvin K. Hedge. That its use is important in distance work is demonstrated by the fact that it is now the standard technique.

'Left Hand Line Acceleration', as it is best termed, gives the caster two great advantages. The first is that the line travels faster and therefore farther, and the second is that the pull on the line, exerting its effect slightly before that of the rod impulse, lifts the end of the straightening line and prevents it touching down either in front or at the rear.

As to the actual timing of the pull with the left hand, even the champions differ. Osten says rod and hand movements begin together, while Hedge and Gregory insist on hand movement just after the start of the rod movement. Edgar May pulls at the same time as he begins his punch and keeps the whole movement as smooth as possible so as to get even acceleration. It is quite possible that all methods are equally effective and are merely individual interpretations to suit the styles of the users. There is little doubt that the hand movement is the first to affect the fly because the forward or backward punch is first expressed as a curve thrown into the butt of the rod. This curve travels up the rod and at the time when the tip is moving fastest the butt is under no stress at all. Shot No16 shows the rod flexed at the butt, while both Nos 5 and 17 show how such a curve reaches the middle and top leaving the butt unflexed. Dick Walker, the well known writer and rod maker, believes that the curve which travels up the rod is reproduced in the line, and I would hazard a guess that he is right. If he is, he has accounted for the wide line loop associated with butt-actioned rods. Shot No9 shows the interesting result of the butt, under the influence of its own momentum, curving backward before the rod has straightened.

I will not say that the method of casting shown in the photographic breakdown accompanying this chapter is easy to learn, few techniques worth mastering ever are, but it is well within the capacity of any angler who has been casting for two seasons and who has learned to keep his left hand moving so as to keep his line tight when punching. Mastery of left hand line acceleration lifts the caster right out of the 'average' class and puts him among the 28 and 30yd men. If the angler goes after the occasional salmon on fairly big rivers he will find that he can cover quite as much water with a 10ft rod as he can with his 12ft greased line rod.

There is an excellent slow motion film, often given at club meetings and dinners, in which Marvin Hedge is shown demonstrating the cast. But even a slow motion film goes too fast for the learner to appreciate what actually happens, and my breakdown was prepared with the need for static shots in mind: shots which can be studied at length.

I know that I have errors of style which limit my distance – most of us have unless we are practising every day under the eye of a good coach – but sometimes we try to correct supposed faults which are not really faults at all. You will notice in several of the shots that I am casting with my finger pointing up the rod. I did so once when casting from the Bedford Casting Club's platform. Afterwards, I said jokingly to Mr J.E.May, 'I suppose I get a reprimand for pointing both thumb and forefinger along the rod?'.

'Why should you?' he replied. 'If you are comfortable casting that way, that is all that matters.'

More and more the coaches of today are concerned that their protégés adopt body positions and styles of action which are comfortable. Most tournament casters get greater power by casting with the right foot forward, but both Godard and Osten cast 'open body' style with left foot forward. Osten adopts this stance so that he can turn his head to watch his line at the rear, a deviation which has always been regarded over here as a serious fault, and equally an unnecessary movement. I do not suggest that all body or rod movements are correct if they are comfortable, but I do suggest that an uncomfortable position cannot be correct.

It is possible that many river anglers, who habitually cast with the right elbow well into the side, may have the idea that merely raising the arm and increasing the effective length of the rod will of itself increase the distance cast. I am afraid they are going to be disillusioned unless they appreciate that a longer rod, or should I say, rod plus extended arm requires greater muscular power, and the real purpose of raising the arm is to enable the muscles from toe to finger to be brought into play.

Throwing a long line demands muscular effort, but when the caster's movements are rhythmic, fatigue is negligible. There is, nevertheless, a limit to the number of false casts the angler can make between 'pick-up' and 'delivery'. Although in tournament casting it is the practice to false-cast until the line is working to the satisfaction of the caster, the fewer the number of false casts the greater the effort which goes into the final forward throw. Quite frequently the tournament caster is able to lift off and throw to the rear; throw forward; throw back, and then throw forward to deliver. It must be remembered, however, that he is using a graphited, free-shooting line which is much heavier in the belly than a No3 double-tapered line. I find that I achieve my best distance which is economical of effort by using the routine shown in the series; if I make an extra false cast my distance is no greater, and often it is rather less.

You will notice that I have worn 'full equipment' while making the casting breakdown. At the time that the shots were taken it was both calm and warm, but I deemed it necessary to prove that this style of casting can be used by the fully accoutred, wading angler as well as by the shirt-sleeved caster on his platform away above the water. The

Plate VI

No 1 With the recovered line bunched in the left hand and some 8 to 10yd of line still unrecovered, the left hand has moved towards the butt-ring and the rod tip has been lowered to the water.

No 2 The rod is extended forward and still. The left hand is drawing line and the rod is about to lift. Hand and rod movements should give even acceleration to the line.

Plate VII

No 3 Rod tip moving fast and fly about to leave the water. The left hand has ceased to move: a short pull on the first back cast makes it easier to feed line back through the rings.

No 4 While line was still moving to the rear, the left hand moved upward feeding line back through the rings in order to decrease distance between hand and butt-ring.

Plate VIII

No 5 The left hand, hauling the line smoothly, has moved away to the left of the body and the rod has punched forward. As the line passes the caster the left hand moves to the position shown in Shot 6.

No 6 The line has passed the caster and the hand has opened to allow line to shoot forward. Note that the rod tip is following the line which will straighten about 5ft above the surface.

Plate IX

No 7 The line has extended forward. As it began to come to rest, the left hand closed to stop line-shoot and moved towards the butt-ring ready for the next haul. This position exists only for an instant.

No 8 From the position shown in Shot 7 the left hand has moved away to the left and the rod has punched to the rear.

Plate X

No 9 A slightly later shot than No 8. Note how the line is assuming the shape of the path of the rod tip. The line is now moving at top speed and the left hand has made the longest possible haul.

No 10 As the line slowed at the rear, the left hand fed line smoothly backwards ready for the second throw forward. The ensuing line haul will move the line before the rod punch affects it.

Plate XI

No 11 Left hand still moving to the left, and rod still flexed. Note that although the butt has moved a long way from its position in Shot 10 the tip has only just started to move.

No 12 The left hand has moved forward and opened to shoot line. Again the rod tip follows the line.

Plate XII

No 13 The last of the 'shoot' was used to decrease distance between hand and butt-ring. The hand is closed and is about to haul with the rod punch to the rear.

No 14 Left hand haul and rod punch have been made; a long line is moving backward. The left hand is already commencing to move upward and the rod is 'drifting' well back ready for maximum effort.

Plate XIII

No 15 Line feeding to the rear.

No 16 A long left hand haul together with the commencing forward punch have thrown a marked curve into the butt. This shot illustrates the demands made of a rod by long casting.

Plate XIV

No 17 Line moving at maximum speed and left hand moving upward to 'shoot'. Note how the whole of the body has assisted in the thrust commenced in Shot 16.

No 18 The final 'shoot' is being made and the left hand is in line with the butt-ring to lessen friction and get the maximum distance. The rod point will follow the falling line.

Plate XV

No 19 Line is being recovered in the left hand, and the rod is at a correct fishing angle. The reader must forgive the caster's grin: he was very relieved to have completed the job in good weather conditions.

Plate XVI

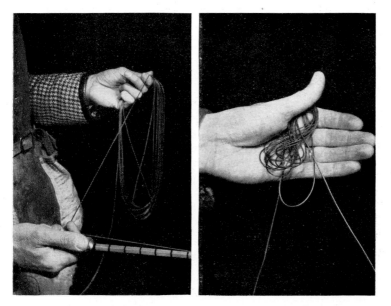

SHOT A: The Coiling Method of line recovery. Note that one loop has gone awry.

SHOT B: The Figure-of-Eight Bunching Method of line recovery.

Plate XVII

SHOT C: Taking the line to commence recovery.

SHOT D: Fingers closed over line. The thumb and fore-finger are being lowered to grip the line at X.

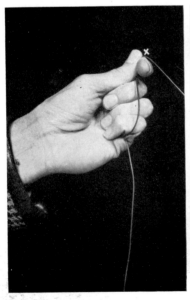

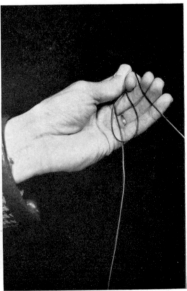

SHOT E: The line at X is seen between the finger and thumb which have now lifted to draw in line.

SHOT F: The second, third and fourth fingers have been withdrawn from the encircling coil shown in 'E' and are placed behind the line as in 'C'. The whole routine is repeated and the line ultimately appears as in 'B'.

length of line and leader used in the series, which is not of course a breakdown of a single cast, was 30½yd, and often enough it all went out on 'delivery'.

Line Recovery

The easiest method is drawing the line over the hooked forefinger of the right hand and dropping it on to the water or the ground. Unfortunately, if you drop it on to the water it often sinks and seriously restricts shooting, while dropping it on to the ground usually results in the line being trodden upon and cut. Obviously, this method of recovery has little to recommend it.

The coiling method of recovery shown in Shot A is often seen in use, and I use it myself when fishing a fly such as the 'Jersey Herd', for it is the fastest of all methods when the line is held in the hand rather than being allowed to drop. When, however, it is necessary to cast a long line and the left hand is used to accelerate, the coils throw over one another and make it difficult to shoot line. Again, it is a fairly frequent occurrence for the coils to jam at the butt-ring when a newly hooked fish runs.

The method shown in Shot B is infinitely superior. It is often referred to as 'W' bunching but since this name is also sometimes applied to a method of winding line between the little finger and thumb I prefer to call it 'Figure-of-Eight-Bunching' since the small coils naturally assume that form. Twenty yards of line can easily be held in the hand, and the line runs free both when shooting and when a fish makes his first rush. In fact I have yet to lose a fish through a figure-of-eight bunched line jamming at the butt-ring.

Shots C, D, E, and F show the breakdown of the movement.

Photographing Casting

There is no gainsaying that you can spot your faults more quickly by studying good action photographs than by any other means. I had always been under the impression that if you enlarged a few frames from a ciné film of casting you would be able to see your every movement and analyse each. In this I was quite wrong; enlargement of ciné shots gives a picture in which movement is blurred and definition very poor. Although I believed it impossible of achievement, Bill Finney soon showed me that a series could be compiled by photographing each required position separately. So good were the results that I asked him to complete some notes on technique, and this he most kindly did for me. The four paragraphs following summarize his conclusions.

A photographic analysis of a cast shows what is actually happening to a rod and line, and this may be different from what the fisherman thinks is happening, or what he hopes is happening. Such an analysis is well within the scope of any keen photographer.

In this case the choice of camera lay between a Rolleiflex at 1/500th, a Leica 111b at 1/1000th and a $3\frac{1}{2} \times 2\frac{1}{2}$ Zeiss Miroflex at 1/2000th. Any of these would have done, but the Miroflex was chosen, largely because its shutter speed was faster than the others, and its negative was reasonable in size. The lens was a 135mm Zeiss Tessar used at its full aperture of f3·5, and the photographs were taken on Kodak P1200 plates, tank developed in Kodak D61a. A camera with a shutter speed lower than 1/500th of a second is practically useless for this work.

One point emerged very clearly during the taking of these pictures. It is quite essential that extremely detailed briefing is given to the photographer, so that he has a mental picture of what he is trying to photograph. Although a cast is quite fast, it is not in the least difficult to open the shutter at exactly the right moment. What is difficult is for a non-fishing photographer to recognize the right moment when he sees it. It was found that the only satisfactory method was for me to make small pencil sketches showing the position of the arms, rod and line at the various stages of the cast, and once this technique was adopted it was quite easy to get the analysis made.

Lastly, if pictures of a perfect cast are wanted, do not waste time taking photographs unless the weather conditions are ideal, particularly in respect of the wind direction and strength. If it is merely required to find out what is actually happening to rod and line under difficult conditions, then this type of photographic 'breakdown' is probably the best way of getting it.

CHAPTER FIVE

....

Flies: A Philosophy

FLIES MAY, BROADLY SPEAKING, be divided into two large families: exact imitations and attractors.

Halford, and other chalk-stream fishermen, established in England a school of thought on flies and fly-tying which has done an incredible amount of harm. When one considers how few Englishmen actually fish the chalk streams, it is amazing that so many books have been written about those rivers. Certain it is that the chalk stream purists have had far too great an influence on English fly design, plugging as they have the exact imitation. I have heard it said that the great Skues was looked upon as a poacher because he dared to fish the nymph form of the fly, though he, too, favoured an exact imitation.

At the risk of disturbing the purist from his dreams of the chalk streams which Plunkett Greene wrote about so beautifully, I must declare that the day of the exact imitation is gone – such flies are a waste of time.

We all differ in our experiences, and our views should always be tempered by these experiences. I have never been failed by the attractors: there has been no occasion to doubt their efficacy, therefore I use them exclusively.

By an 'exact imitation', I mean an artificial fly which has the same form, translucency, flash, size and perhaps sex as the natural.

Let us be honest about it. How many of us can ever be satisfied with our exact imitations, having seen the real thing? Do they not by their failings – however clever we may be – fill us with doubt as to whether or not the fish will sneer at them as they pass them by? Of course they do. How then can we fish well with them when we lack the first essential: complete faith in the fly we are using.

The adage has it, that 'It ain't what you do; it's the way that you do it.' Applied to fishing, I would phrase it, 'It ain't what you fish, it's the way that you fish it.'

The logical deduction from that paraphrase is that the style of fishing is of paramount and the fly of only secondary importance. Continuing from this point we reach the conclusion, that we cannot decide on a fly until we know by what method we are going to fish. In its turn the decision as to method depends upon such things as light, wind, season and the way the fish are seen to behave.

We have most of us at some time or other seen a wet-fly cast made up with say, an Alexandra on the tail and a nymph on the dropper. How can such a combination be effective? Only one of the flies can be fished at one time, for flies like the Alexandra must be fished fast, while a nymph or spider must move only fast enough to appear alive.

We have arrived at a convenient point to differentiate between the two types of attractors, namely: the 'flashers' which include such patterns as Peter Ross, Butcher and Alexandra; and the 'deceivers' such as Greenwell's Glory, Tup's, and my Black and Peacock Spiders, all three of which bear a superficial resemblance to many insects and other water creatures.

I believe that although a trout may take a well-presented 'imitation', it will more readily accept a well-fished 'deceiver'. The fish accepts the latter as a different food species and is not concerned to compare it with the natural on the water at the time. How otherwise do we explain consistent refusal of an imitation followed by immediate and confident seizing of a great 'fuzzy-buzzy' which does not in the slightest resemble any God-created water animal? I admit the existence of the 'daft 'un', and the 'bloody-minded' fish, but the experience I have just referred to occurs far too frequently to be ascribed justifiably to either of these two causes entirely.

Perhaps the greatest error made in the fishing of our Midland reservoirs is dry-fly fishing. Looking over my diary, which records weather and light conditions, the success of others as well as my own takes or blanks (and these last occur more frequently than I would like), I find that I have taken only six fish on the dry-fly in the last five years. I have on many occasions given up the whole of a rise to test the worth of dry-flies. On other occasions I have fished wet near to another successful angler who was fishing dry. The results of tests, fairly conducted by several of us, prove that the wet-fly is far and away more deadly than the dry-fly, even in a rise.

The key to the situation lies in the behaviour of the fish.

Unlike river trout, our fish do not take up a 'lie' and feed on creatures on or below the surface carried down to them by the current. In slack water, they are free to move about, and in fact spend their lives doing so, feeding as they move on a wide variety of food forms: seldom are they selective. These fish do not grow to be 2½lb [1] at as little as four years by feeding on dry-fly, in fact, the wonder to me is that we see them rise to surface-food at all. When we perform an autopsy, we find the gut full of snail (I have taken fish which rattled when you shook them) mixed with various larval insects, water-boatmen, and later in the season, sticklebacks in large numbers.

1. Such fish are, of course, exceptional; usually the four-year-old will weigh about 1lb 2oz.

There is little incentive to fish to rise when the bottom provides such rich feeding, so why persist in fishing dry, when for every creature taken at the surface at least forty must be taken below it. Again, although a dry-fly can be worked, it soon loses its buoyancy, particularly in a ripple. Yet work the fly we must, in order to cover as much water as possible, for as we have said, the trout are on the move, and are not confined to a lie over which we can float the fly at will. However we look at the matter, the practical answer is the wet-fly.

Just before the opening of the 1951 season I had a letter from a fisherman whom I had occasionally seen on the local waters. He asked for advice. He said he had come to the conclusion that although he had always fished dry he ought to change to wet-fly, which was, he believed, a far more difficult form of fishing. His belief is correct.

In wet-fly work the angler is concerned with the things he cannot see, and his fly works in an extra dimension: depth. He must know, or find out by trial and error (or hunch based on experience), what speed of fishing and therefore what fly will give the best results at the required depth. I took my fastest limit, four fish weighing 11lb 10oz in thirty minutes without having seen a fish rise but having a shrewd idea where they were and what they were doing. Like John Moore's colonel who could think like a goose, we must try to think like our quarry, the trout.

As I expected, my earlier references to dry-fly fishing caused a great deal of perturbation and botheration. Significantly, most of the critics who felt dry-fly had been unfairly condemned were men who lived in Wales. Many of the Welsh reservoirs are oligotrophic waters, deficient in bottom feed. Fish in such waters rise to fly relatively freely because the natural is an important part of their diet. It has been most noticeable that men such as Ernest Phillips, Myles-Tonks, 'Mayfly' and others who know Midland waters well, share my views and endorse the majority of my conclusions. Of the many letters received only one referred to a selective rise and this was stated to occur at Durleigh Reservoir to a chironomus variety. I have not experienced it myself.

It must be remembered that my aim is to show how fish may best be caught; I am concerned to help the reader to avoid blanks, and that I can do by advising him to avoid the use of the dry-fly.

Although I have stressed the necessity for fishing the fly in an attractive manner, it is obvious that some patterns are more attractive than others. At one time I would cheerfully have gone out with only the Black and Peacock Spider dressed in several sizes. But the following season it failed badly and I had to evolve alternatives.

In my box at the moment I admit I count twenty-eight different patterns. On only twelve of them have I caught fish, and according to my records four patterns have accounted for 85 per cent of my fish while eight patterns have accounted for just under 96 per cent. It is these eight patterns which I shall deal with in detail in my next chapter.

I often ask myself why I bother to tie other patterns, and the only answer, I fear, is vanity. They do look so nice in the box; they satisfy my eye; they provide me with an opportunity to demonstrate a very little skill at fly-tying. These non-fishing flies, by the way, were never created until I had passed the novice stage as a fly-tyer, and I would suggest that when a fisherman reaches this stage he is in a very great danger of beginning to overdress his flies. I have avoided the danger by tying two sorts of flies, those for me and those for the fish, and it is not a bad principle.

And what of the hooks we use?

There is one pattern which stands out above all others. It is similar to that used by Messrs Hardy Bros and is supplied by Messrs Messeena as 'Pattern 106', and by Messrs Veniard as 'Wide Gape Trout'. It is a grand hook: the wire is light, the point is sharp and short, the wide gape gives it a good deep hold (in flesh) and the tempering is perfect.

The trout is hard-mouthed, and long-pointed hooks often hit bone before they are 'in over the barb'. In lake fishing, the head of the taking fish may be pointing in almost any direction when the strike is made, and hooking in the 'scissors' of the jaws happens in only about 20 per cent of cases. For the remainder, the hook may be anywhere inside or outside the mouth and 'skin-nicking' is common, hence my insistence on short points. The short-pointed hook goes in over the barb, even in skin over a bony surface, and thus gives one a decided advantage.

The size of the hooks is of great importance. When a large fish heads for a weed-bed there are four things which can happen. You can stop the fish, or, more probably, the fish achieves his object. On the other hand your cast may part or your hook may tear free. It is this last possibility I am concerned with now.

Large hooks, being made of thicker wire than small hooks, have less tendency to cut the flesh and thus enlarge the hole; in addition their initial hold is much deeper. I have fished with small hooks and taken several fish on them, but I am worried from the moment I strike to the moment the fish is lost or netted, because I know that I can never apply full pressure and that every turn of the fish is loosening a hold which can never be truly secure unless it is in the 'scissors'. I lost the largest trout I have ever hooked (the fish mentioned in

Chapter 2) solely, I believe, because I used a hook smaller than could reasonably be expected to hold for the duration of a long fight!

The basic size of hook for use on reservoirs containing large fish is a size 7 (new scale) during early spring, and a 6 from mid-May onwards when the light is more brilliant. The largest size I use is a 9, and the smallest under normal conditions is a 4.

I have used a size 0 hook and have taken a fish of 2lb 13oz on one, but on the other hand I have also pricked so many other fish and lost them that I now never use anything less than a 3.

Small hooks and fine gut are not fair fishing. Rising fish are sufficiently hard to find without decreasing their number by pricking and losing them, an experience which must tend to discourage fish from feeding near the surface.

A day when I rise ten fish and take only my four, perhaps pricking the others as does sometimes happen, is not a satisfying day. We should all aim to hook and net every fish we rise, and we ought not to take risks which preclude the possibilities of doing this. I notice that at Blagdon, spinning with lines under 4lb breaking strain is not permitted. Although a single hook left in a fish does less damage than a treble, neither event is desirable. You cannot cast a large hook on a fine gut point, and a small hook will not work properly when constrained by a stout cast, thus, you either must fish safely or take two risks: fine gut and small hooks.

I believe that when waters are known to contain a large number of very heavy fish, the rules ought to lay down minimum sizes for both casts and flies, but until that happens our common sense and good sportmanship must suffice.

CHAPTER SIX

Some Useful Fly-Dressings

I STARTED FLY-DRESSING for the very prosaic reason that I could not afford to lose flies at 9s per dozen, their price when I returned home at the end of the war. How grateful I am now that my pocket was not better filled, for I would have missed a lot of fun and the additional satisfaction of taking fish on my own handiwork. I would also have caught far fewer fish, and that is a point that concerns us all.

Last season I had killed a fish and was in the process of weighing him when E.G. came along to help me gloat over him.

'What did you get him on,' he asked, 'another one of your bare hook shanks? I'm damned if I know why the fish take 'em.'

I think his question and remark should be studied by every firm tying flies, particularly the Midlands and London fly dressers.

One famous London firm were the tyers of an Alexandra which was given to me some years ago. It had so much dressing on it that it would not sink until it was given a good sharp pull, and it was tied on a heavy-wire Limerick hook at that. The North Country fly-dressers tie flies which will catch fish without the prior removal of more than 25 per cent of the dressing, but it is much easier to dress your own flies and have them correct to start with. Since we shall not be tying to very small hooks, great skill is not necessary. Two very successful angler friends of mine tie the most horrible monstrosities I have ever seen – one dressing is known to us all as the 'Pregnant Nymph', and that is a pretty fair name and description. Nevertheless, crude as many of their dressings are, they catch fish, and that will always be the acid test of a fly.

The essentials of a good wet-fly are, that it shall sink readily, its hackle-fibres shall be soft and sparse, and its wing very narrow (if there at all) and tied to lie low over the body. The whole fly should be light and sparkling – never opaque – in silhouette against the trout's window.

It has been something of a disappointment to me that I have had so many enquiries about colours of herls and flosses etc, and so few, relatively, on methods of fishing the flies.

My flies are now tied, excellently, and marketed by Messrs Walker, Bampton. Nevertheless I will repeat what I said in Chapter 5, that method is if anything more important than the fly pattern used.

A very kind friend who had read and appreciated what I had written, presented me with a copy of the 1851 edition of Pulman's *Vade Mecum of Fly-Fishing for Trout*. I read few fishing books and Pulman was a stranger to me. You may well picture my surprise when having read in Chapter 7 of the follies of exact imitation I came across the following passage:

'But supposing this to be otherwise, – supposing even the angler to be an expert, and to have a good imitation of the fly at which the fish are rising well, – say a fly of the dun tribe, prevalent on every water. He makes his cast admirably. In the gentle stickle which hugs the opposite bank, a line of trout are rising gloriously; but not one of them is attracted by his well presented lure. He throws, and throws again, but still with the same result. He is at a loss to account for the cause, except that it must evidently be something or other wrong in his fly. No such thing. We admit the fly to be a good imitation, to be nicely cast over rising fish, repeatedly, time after time, and yet with not a rise, is poor Piscator favoured. Well, how is this? Piscator does not see – he is so wrapped up in the make of his fly – that something more than make is necessary; that under certain circumstances an imitation of the action of the natural fly is indispensable, and that when that action is not supplied, as in the present case, success cannot be had.'

A hundred years in our history as a nation has seen many changes. But Mother Nature's trout have let time pass by them; today they behave just as they did in Pulman's time.

Here then are my best eight patterns, and may they do for you what they have done for me! The first seven patterns will be strangers to most readers, but the eighth is an old favourite suitably dressed for our purpose. The remarks on the methods of fishing each pattern are, as I have said, more important than the patterns themselves, since the methods could be applied to any fly of a weight and form such that it would be likely to behave in a similar manner in the water.

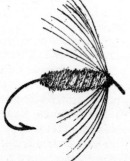

THE BLACK AND PEACOCK SPIDER

33

Tie-in three or four strands of bronze peacock herl and a strand of any dark silk floss at bend of hook; carry tying-silk back to the head. Wind a floss underbody, slender at the tail and fairly thick in the thorax, and tie-off the floss at head. Twist the strands of herl together in anti-clockwise direction and wind the body in clockwise direction; tie-off. Tie-in a relatively large, soft-fibred, black hen hackle by the stub, with the underside of the feather facing the bend of the hook; take two turns only and tie-off. (Hackles for this and the following dressing should never be doubled.) The hackle should stand out as shown in the diagram. Whip finish and varnish. This pattern should be tied in sizes 4, 5, 6, 7 and 8 (new scale); sizes 6, and 7 are the most useful.

This fly is the best all-rounder in my box. I have taken fish on it under every type of weather condition. It should be fished very slowly at all times. When small black snails are seen on the stones of the dams it is particularly good (remember the snail comes to the surface and drifts with the foot uppermost while breathing). The fly also does very well when the fish first begin to feed on fry. In addition, it is the only pattern on which I have taken fish in the crazy Silverhorn rise at the back-end of the season. During very bright weather I have used a deep-sinking variation of this pattern on a 12ft cast, with great success. The peacock body is over-wound with ·012 nylon – leaving a short space between each turn. Being wholly submerged, the cast is almost invisible, and line-wake (never entirely absent in calm water) is sufficiently remote from the deep-fishing fly not to worry the fish.

During the evening rise, when the back fins of the fish break water as they take with little disturbance, the Black and Peacock Spider is very deadly fished on a cast greased down to the last 18in. The fish themselves are often moving only about a foot below the surface, and it is essential that your fly shall fish between 2in and 6in from the surface. Because the wake of the cast will only be about 17in from the fly, you must draw more slowly than at any other time.

Many fishermen are afraid to draw slowly, so I will try to explain the theory of the practice.

If you watch a few square feet of clear shallow water you will notice that the small water-creatures move a matter of only 3in or 4in in as many seconds. It is true that on a river your fly travels from A, across stream, to B, downstream, quite quickly. But relative to the water which carries it, the fly moves scarcely at all (I presume the line was mended and that there has been no 'drag'). Perhaps the rapid travelling of the river-fly is responsible for the idea that many lake fishermen have, that their flies should travel over the ground at a similarly high speed. Certainly, this would account for the fast 'cast and lift' method so prevalent in lake or loch fishing. When we examine a maker's lake flies we find that with few exceptions they are 'flashers', for the 'deceiver' patterns are quite useless when fished fast.

The fast-moving, flashing fly tends to rouse the 'lust to kill' in large fish; on the other hand such flies quite often scare fish out of the area. Surely it is easier to achieve success by appealing to the instinct which is seldom dormant: the feeding instinct. Under normal conditions, then, I strongly advise you to use 'deceiver' patterns, confining the use of 'flashers' to the special circumstances mentioned in the paragraphs on 'flasher' dressings.

Already the Black and Peacock Spider has proved its worth to others. Flight Lieutenant L.A.R. Hunt and 'Mayfly' (W.J. Thomas) had excellent sport with it during the back-end of the 1951 season at Durleigh Reservoir, Somerset. I feel, too, that it will prove an answer to the rise to the Corixa at Blagdon.

THE GREEN NYMPH

Tie-in white floss and pale green nylon monofilament at bend of hook (the nylon should be ·009in for size 4 hooks, increasing to ·014in at size 8; the whitish nylons absorb dye very readily). The nylon strand is more easily tied in if the end is first knotched between the teeth. Whip tying-silk back to ⅛in from eye. Wind floss underbody, making thorax slightly thicker, and tie-off. Wind nylon closely to ⅛in from eye, and tie-off. Tie-in brown partridge hackle and wind on two turns, then tie-off. Now tie-in two strands of bronze peacock herl; twist together as before; wind about four turns to form a largish head in front of the hackle and tie-off. Whip finish and varnish.

This fly is heavy and is therefore ideal when deep sinking is required or when very small flies must be used. During May and June when big hatches of fly take place, there are many hours of the day when not a move is to be seen. This is particularly true on days of flat calm when no land insects are blown on to the water. The fish are there all right, and they are feeding, but not near the surface. They will be found wherever there is an open mud bottom with 4ft or 5ft of water over it, and they will be gorging nymph. Use as long a cast as you can handle, and ensure that the gut or nylon will sink readily by removing the grease with soap, or with a moistened pad on which a little of one of the new detergents such as 'Dreft' has been sprinkled. Never use clay or mud as I so often see advised in print. Be careful to rinse surplus soap from your finger-tips before touching your line, for soap will sink your line quite as efficiently as it does your cast. Now, make your cast and allow the fly at least twenty seconds to sink to the bottom; with rod point high, say, at half past ten o'clock, draw the line 6in and rest a second; repeat until ready to lift and cast again. Watch the knot where line joins cast and strike the moment you see it draw away. Often enough, the first you will know of a fish anywhere near at hand will be a smash take, when your rod will almost leave your hand, hence the high rod-tip. Of course, you will feel more fish take if you hold the rod-tip down to the water and point the rod down the line, but you will have far more breaks, too. By the way, the 'smash take' seems always to come just when you have decided that there are no fish about, or when you are watching something other than your line.

It is easy to concentrate on a river, but the habit is difficult to acquire on still water. Lack of concentration will cost you many fish at first.

THE BROWN NYMPH

Strip the flue from two strands of green-dyed ostrich herl and tie-in at bend of hook; tie-in oval gold tinsel and one strand of brown-dyed ostrich herl; carry tying-silk back to ⅛in from eye. Wind ostrich herl body and tie-off; rib with tinsel and tie-off. Carry green quill direct from the bend, over the upper side of body to the head and tie-off. Tie-in two strands of peacock herl; twist together and wind about four turns behind the eye to form a head and tie-down. Now separate the two strands and carry them backwards to form horns, and tie-down in the position shown in diagram; tie-off. Whip finish and varnish.

This fly is lighter than the Green Nymph and consequently fishes in the middle or upper part of the water. It is excellent when fish are taking nymphs as they come to the surface, although I must admit I have had as great success with the Black and Peacock Spider when this is happening. Again, you must fish it slowly and be ready for smash takes well below the surface of the water. Both the Green and

Brown Nymphs should be tied in sizes 4, 5, 6 and 7; sizes 5 and 6 are the most useful.

THE GREEN AND YELLOW NYMPH

Tie-in two strands of green-dyed swan herl at bend; carry silk back to half-way up the shank. Wind green herl to middle of shank and tie-off. Tie-in two strands deep yellow-dyed swan herl; carry silk to ⅛in from eye of hook. Wind yellow herl to ⅛in from eye and tie-off. Tie-in two strands of peacock herl; wind head as for Green Nymph; tie-off; whip finish and varnish.

This fly should be tied in sizes 4, 5 and 6; sizes 4 and 5 being most useful. The fly fishes high in the water, and should be used when fish are nymphing just beneath the surface or are taking the surface fly.

THE BROWN AND GREEN NYMPH

Tie-in four strands of peacock herl by their tips, leaving the tips pointing aft as a tail ¼in long. Tie-in one strand of green-dyed ostrich herl, one of brown-dyed ostrich herl, and oval gold tinsel at bend, and carry tying-silk back to ⅛in from eye. Wind green and brown herl together to form a segmented body of alternate colours and tie-off. Rib with tinsel and tie-off. Carry peacock herl direct to the head over the back and tie-down. Now twist the strands of peacock herl together; wind three or four turns to form a bold head and tie-off. Whip finish and varnish.

I tie this fly in sizes 5 to 8, leaded and unleaded. I use it as a change fly for the Green Nymph and the Brown Nymph and it has always killed well. I have also used it very successfully on 'sticklebackers', fished both slowly and fast, probably because the fly is somewhat minnowish in appearance. And now we come to the 'flasher' patterns.

The 'Pretty-Pretty' is a fly which seems to satisfy the eye of both fish and fisherman. The tying is quite orthodox and I will merely give it as a specification.

Tag, silver tinsel; tail, small golden pheasant topping feather;

underbody, floss silk; body, peacock herl and green-dyed ostrich herl twisted together (the excellent effect of this mixture when wet has to be seen to be believed); ribbing, oval silver tinsel; hackle, two turns of green-dyed hen hackle; wing, goat-hair dyed orange-yellow.

THE 'PRETTY-PRETTY'

I tie this pattern in sizes 6, 7, 8 and 9; size 8 being the most useful size. This fly must be fished fast and therefore must be tied to sink very readily. Too much goat hair will make it surface and render it useless.

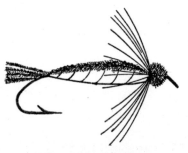

THE 'JERSEY HERD'

Take a size 9 (new scale) long-shank trout hook (these can be obtained from Messrs Veniard) or alternatively a size 6 Low Water Salmon hook, though these do not drive home so easily as trout hooks. Tie-in floss-silk at bend, and wind a bold underbody which thickens at the centre of the shank, fly-minnow fashion. Now tie-in wide, copper-coloured, flat tinsel or alternatively a strip of milk-cap foil, and about twelve strands of bronze peacock herl, leaving the tips of the herl pointing aft to form a tail about $\frac{5}{16}$in long. Carry your tying-silk to $\frac{3}{16}$in from the eye; wind your tinsel as for an Alexandra, and tie-down at head. Carry the herl over the upper side of the body and tie-down. Tie-in a doubled, short-fibred cock hackle dyed a rich orange; take two turns and tie-down. Now twist the strands of peacock herl together in an anti-clockwise direction and take two turns in front of the hackle to form a bold head. Tie off and whip finish.

This pattern should be tied both leaded and unleaded. I found that when using the leaded pattern it was necessary to use a point up to ·014in in diameter for the sake of ease of control in casting. Although so thick a point would seem to be so conspicuous as to alarm fish; this does not occur in practice, for the fly must be fished very fast. If fished slowly it is a failure, even when ·010in points are used. Some idea of the speed at which the fly must be fished will be gathered by my statement that it is impossible to recover line fast enough by normal 'figure-of-eight' bunching in the left hand. Much as I dislike doing it I resort to coiling my line when fishing the 'Jersey Herd'.

It may be said with some justice that 'stripping through' is nearer to spinning than it is to fly fishing, but under difficult conditions on a reservoir you will never be blamed for using any method or fly which is within the rules. In any case, there is no denying that the 'Jersey Herd' is a very minnowish creation, it most certainly does not resemble a fly any more than do the Peter Ross and Alexandra.

There is an interesting history to this 'fly'. During Whit-week, 1951 I was on the water almost every day. 1951 was a crazy season, with fish migrations within the reservoir taking place three weeks later than is normal. In April instead of being off the dam, we found the fish were still in the marginal shallows. During Whit-week when they should have been back on the shallows they were feeding off the dam and the shallows were hopeless.

On Whit-Monday several anglers took fish off the dam while using Alexandras or other 'monstrosities', but I noticed that other anglers on the dam who fished with normal-sized flies caught nothing, and I concluded that it was a matter of using a fly which could be fished fast without its coming to the surface.

We had stiff northerly winds blowing straight into the dam all the week. The usual 9ft 6in, heavy centre, McClane taper cast would not cope with the conditions, and I resorted to a 7ft 6in cast, tapered steeply from ·020in down to ·011in. Even size 9 (new scale) Alexandras and Pretty-Pretties were too light to stay down, and merely skated across the top, so severe was line-drag.

That evening I produced a really heavy large fly of a type which E.N. and A.L. had occasionally used in 1950. I used this fly to the exclusion of all else on the Wednesday, Thursday and Friday, and took a limit of two brace on each day. Other, and successful, anglers persisting with normal 'flasher' patterns accounted for odd fish only. There was no question of superior skill: weather conditions demanded fast recovery, and my fly was heavy enough to stay submerged while I stripped through.

This fly is now a permanent addition to my box. I have used it on many occasions, under conditions varying from a heavy 'lop' down to flat calm, and I have never failed to rise a fish with it. As you would expect, in July and August and during calms the fish tended to chase it without actually taking it; that, too, can be turned to good account. On several occasions, having thus found a fish, I rested him, and then 'flogged' him and took him with a nymph fished deep. The fly was first tied with copper-coloured foil from a bottle of Jersey-herd milk, and I therefore named the fly 'The Jersey Herd'.

The last of my eight is the 'flasher' supreme: The Alexandra. I usually tie this fly with oval silver ribbing over the flat tinsel body to increase the flash. I never use more than eight strands of herl for winging large sizes, and only three or four strands for size 4 hooks. A Golden × Amherst pheasant topping feather completes the dressing.

This fly is useful in all sizes from 4 to 9.

I have known the Alexandra to be used successfully in size 0 and 00, fished slowly near the surface in conditions of brilliant light, but I do not advise it: far more fish will be pricked and lost than ever will be netted.

The chief limitation of 'flashers' is that they have no normal application under conditions of flat calm: the use of the 'Jersey Herd' for searching out a fish during July or August is exceptional. In the ordinary course of events flashers must only be used when there is sufficient ripple to break up the wake of the line. They must be fished fast in order to disguise their tinsel and feather origin, and at the necessary speed in flat calm the line, and sometimes the fly, leave a wake like a motor torpedo-boat.

Small wonder the loch-fisherman, limited to the standard loch flies and methods, prays for a stiff breeze and rippled surface.

Although the deceivers will always be my first choice, possibly because of the delicacy with which they must be fished as much as the excellent bags they make possible, there is one occasion when 'flashers' must be used.

In strong cross-winds the line will develop a deep belly downwind. This drawback can be overcome, in part, by putting the rod point over, but the only fully satisfactory remedy is to use 'flashers' and fish fast and thus keep in touch with your fly. There is only one occasion when you may safely be out of touch with your fly, and that is when you are able to see your cast, or the knot at the loop of the cast. It is only in winds of from 15mph upwards (at 90° to your line) that the 'flasher' is absolutely necessary. Below that speed the deceiver can be used, but you must cast a shorter line and pick up before a deep belly in the line occurs.

I well realize that throughout the book I have been using such loose terms as 'slow', 'fast', 'medium speed' and so on. Speed is important since it affects both the depth of a fly and its power to deceive. I have therefore carried out a series of time trials under actual fishing conditions to establish the speeds at which I use the patterns of flies given in this chapter. My line was marked at 21½yd, and a 3½yd cast was attached making a total of 25yd. The 10ft 'Iron Murderer' was used in the experiments and the pick-up was made when the cast loop was 6in from the tip, that is, when the fly was 7yd away from me. Thus 18yd of line was recovered after making each 25yd cast. The times for recovery given in the table below are the average of five separate recoveries for each pattern.

Speed	Fly pattern	Method of recovery	Time	
Normal	All nymphs	'Figure-of-Eight' bunching	2 min	13 sec
Slow	„ „	„ „ „ „	2 min	40 sec
Normal	Black and Peacock Spider	„ „ „ „	1 min	28 sec
Slow	„ „ „ „	„ „ „ „	1 min	42 sec
Normal	Alexandra and 'Pretty-Pretty'	„ „ „ „	1 min	2 sec
Fast	„ „ „ „	„ „ „ „		44 sec
Normal	'Jersey Herd'	Coiling		35 sec
Fast	„ „	„		28 sec

I have had several letters from anglers who want to know how I manage to fish both deep and fast simultaneously when using ordinary 'flasher' patterns.

Quite obviously one cannot fish as deep when fishing fast as when fishing slowly, but taken by and large a fly tends to remain at a fairly even depth during recovery, particularly if you can exert a horizontal pull on it.

Putting two and two together, I am fairly convinced that several of those who wrote have attempted to fish fast while using a cast consisting of a 3yd long parallel length of nylon. Such a cast must always exert an upward pull on the fly. By lengthening the cast the direction of pull on the fly is more nearly horizontal, but a 4yd long length of monofil is unmanageable. The secret is to have a weight some distance above the fly, and the weight you use is the ·020in length of nylon in the heavy-centre casts given in Chapter 3.

Stokes' Law has it that the rate of fall of a body in a fluid varies as the square of the radius. In common parlance 'the thicker the length of nylon, the quicker it sinks'. Applied to heavy-centred casts, the law means that the heavy-centre will tend to lie lower in the water than the nylon next the fly.

Cast design may appear to be a detail, but it is attention to such details which makes the difference between success and failure. I used to think the deep sinking at the centre of a double-tapered cast was a disadvantage. How wrong I was! I am certain that it is the use of these casts, exerting an almost horizontal pull on the fly, which enables me to do the 'impossible' – namely, to fish my fly fast, and keep it at the depth to which I allow it to sink before beginning to recover line.

That Vexed Question!

Despite my own views on dry-fly fishing, I realize that many anglers will want to fish 'dry' from time to time.

Perhaps it is labouring the point to suggest that the primary requirement of a dry-fly is that it shall float. Nevertheless there are many dry-flies sold which are very deficient in this respect.

In river fishing, the fly, relative to the water, remains stationary; in still-water fishing the fly is worked, and normally dressed patterns readily become waterlogged.

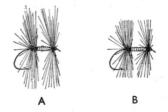

A   B

Flies dressed as in the diagram float much better than the single-hackled patterns. If necessary you can tell yourself that you are dressing the 'knotted' imago. Tie-in two stiff hackles from a Brown Leghorn Cock-neck, at the bend of the hook. Wind to form a good bushy hackle and tie-off. Tie-in a piece of oval gold tinsel and wind it as a body to about $\frac{3}{16}$in from the eye. Tie-in two more hackle feathers and wind the front hackle. Tie-off; whip finish and varnish head.

If you prefer it, the front hackle can be of another colour and your fly thus becomes a type of 'Bi-visible'.

These dry flies can be dressed on hooks from size 3 to 8. The floating powers seem to be improved by clipping the hackle as shown in 'B' of the above diagram. Such 'Fuzzy Buzzy' dressings in large sizes can be used as 'Wake' flies in the gloaming; but having used them for this purpose I can say that a Black and Peacock Spider catches more fish.

Fly-Dressing Materials

It is seldom necessary to buy expensive plumage. Many highly coloured feathers are a chalky white in reverse and nowhere nearly so efficient as dyed material. When dying, plumage should be stripped of soft fibre and down feathers, tied in small bundles and thoroughly cleansed of grease in *warm* soapy water. Cleaning should be followed by thorough rinsing and the feathers should be placed in the dye-bath, wet, to ensure even dyeing. The dyes I use are the ordinary six-penny 'Fairy' Dyes and I use them at about 180°F. The colour should be checked frequently by lifting the bundle by the attached cotton and rinsing in clean water. If you are dying to a pattern, wet the pattern thoroughly so as to make a fair comparison.

Nylon is dyed in the same way, but after the soap washing requires thirty minutes' soaking in warm water, it will then readily absorb the dye. The grey Continental nylons do not dye so well as the white English and American nylons.

Ostrich herl and other plumage used for body making should always be dyed on the quill.

Hackle feathers should be obtained on the skin whenever possible: they are thus already graded for size. If you see a bird with the required neck plumage hanging at a poulterer's shop, ask him to cut the neck skin off for you. At home open the skin and tack it stretched on to a board with the flesh side uppermost. Scrape off as much fat and flesh as you can and merely leave the skin to dry. I have read of rubbing alum into the skins but I have never done so myself and I have two neck skins quite five years old in my box of plumage and in perfect preservation.

Some sellers of tying materials supply herl, hair and like materials as a shapeless mixture packed loose in an envelope. Why they do it I do not know, but I loathe the practice. Materials of this type should always be supplied on the quill or on the skin.

Hair will gradually replace feather as a winging material for many patterns, and there is every reason to suppose the result will be a better fly. Many feather-fibre wings are opaque, hair wings 'work' in a wonderfully life-like manner and are translucent.

When you start to use hair a whole new field of sources of supply is opened up. I recall that a few years ago I found an excellent 'Brown and Grizzled' mixture for Low Water 'March Brown' wings, on the flanks of a good looking collie. The dog didn't need that hair half so much as I did!

CHAPTER SEVEN

....

Raw Spring Days

I HAVE ALWAYS ATTEMPTED to elevate fishing to the plane of an exact science. The man who *thinks* 'fish and fishing' must ultimately succeed in catching more fish than the man who believes in leaving it to luck. And yet, until the middle of May, the element of chance in reservoir trout fishing cannot be relegated to a back seat.

The whole of the trouble appears to me to centre around the fact that when the season opens some fish are in good condition, others barely recovered from spawning, while some are still heavy with spawn. In other words the fish as a whole have not settled down to a predictable pattern of behaviour.

I would like to quote some results which tend to illustrate my point.

Tuesday, 11 May 1948. Four fish taken, 1lb 4oz, 1lb 6oz, 1lb 12oz and 2lb 8oz. The first three were fat as butter and were probably fish which had spawned for the first time. Scale-readings of similar fish taken in 1951 tend to support this conclusion. The first spawning of brown trout is seldom an exhausting process. The 2½lb fish was 18in long and had a girth of 10½in. The ovaries were well developed and there were two or three unabsorbed ova in the abdominal cavity, proving she had spawned during the previous winter. Her flesh was pink and firm. At 2pm on the same day, E.N. took a hen fish weighing 5lb 8oz and which contained about 1½lb of unshed ova.

Saturday, 9 April 1949. I took one fish weighing 2lb 15oz and which was 22½in long. She came ashore writhing like an eel and was promptly returned to the water. The fish, by the way, was smutting and I took her on a size 4 Black and Peacock Spider. Strange what fish will do!

Friday, 7 April 1950. Two fish were taken, the larger weighing 2lb 5oz was thin and had the sunken flank indicating recent spawning. The following day also saw me with two fish, the larger of which again weighed 2lb 5oz. This fish was, however, in really excellent condition.

Many more such examples could be given of these early season contrasts in condition, but these should suffice.

I suggest we go fishing on a really bleak opening day and solve our problems as we meet them.

Plate XVIII

Whenever the wind sets into the dam fish will be found quite close in to the margin and the casting procedure discussed in Chapter 7 will give good results. It was under such conditions that the 'Jersey Herd' gave such good results in 1951.

The first thing we notice as we arrive and surrender our permits is that the water is about 11ft higher than it was when we left it last season. In fact, with a 15mph to 20mph wind setting towards the outflow, water is pouring over, as waves nearly 2ft high break against its concrete and brickwork lip.[1]

As usual we tackle-up down by the boathouse. We seem to be the first arrivals, which is just as well, or we would have been yarning till 10am of last year's notable deeds.

We meet with no snags assembling our gear, nor should we after six long 'black' months, with time and to spare for tackle repairs. The sky is leaden, and what is more important, the water is very rough, which means we shall have to fish fast and use flashers of size 7 or larger. I shall therefore use a 9ft 6in cast with a heavy centre tapering to ·011in. Normally, I would use ·010in, but under these conditions a size larger will make no difference to the fish, who are anything but 'educated' at the moment.

I do not know whether or not you like to fish a dropper; I some-times do early in the season when the weeds are dormant, but I shall not use one today. Two flies increase the wind resistance of the leader and thus make casting more difficult.

These large fish often follow the fly for many yards before taking, and I doubt if I have taken more than ten fish in the last five years on a dropper. In a deep water when the trout are well down the chances are that if they see the dropper they will also see the tail fly, and since with a long line the dropper does not work as a 'bob' fly, there is no advantage in fishing a dropper. In shallow water it is quite possible that a fish may see only one of the flies, and a dropper then may give results, but the dropper truly comes into its own only when nymphing – a subject for future treatment.

I suggest we give them an alternative diet; you try a 'Pretty-Pretty' and I will start with an Alexandra. There is usually a fish to be found in the corner where the dam and bank meet, and we may as well start there.

So close to the dam; if we drop our flies about 80ft from the margin they will be over 6ft to 8ft of water – a useful depth at this time of

1. By contrast, the opening day of the 1952 season saw the beginning of an un-seasonably warm spell. In spite of water temperature of only 44°F, we had a series of evening rises such as the water keeper had not seen so early in the season during his twenty-five years' experience. Fish refused a fly sunk more than 2in and many wet-fly fishermen, not realizing what was happening, and unable to get fish on a wet-fly 12in or more below the surface changed to dry-fly and then took fish. I found the answer to their behaviour when my first three fish of the season were taken on a dropper. Fishing greased cast from then onwards, as explained in the next chapter, proved the solution, and the wet-fly again showed itself master of every situation.

year. Fishing this spot will help us to deal with one of the problems of wind.

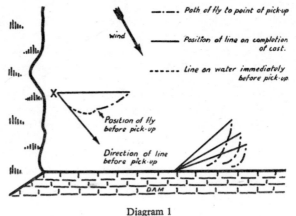

Diagram 1

This diagram shows our position relative to the corner of the dam.

As we cast from X, at 90° to the bank, the wind is blowing at 60° to the line and forming a deep belly, so we hold our rods parallel to the water and at 110° to the line, as in Diagram 2, to cut out the belly of line between rod-tip and water. The belly of line on the water, plus the rod at an angle to the line, will prevent a breakage if we have a heavy 'take'.

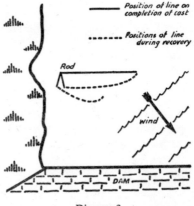

Diagram 2

Fanning our casts enables us to cover all the water within reach, but after half an hour has passed we have not seen, felt or heard anything of a fish, and so, having got the 'feel' of our rods again, we decide to tackle the difficult conditions of the dam.

Early in the season when the fish require heavy feeding to regain condition after spawning, they lie in deep water where there is an abundance of snail. The steep gradient of the dam offers us our readiest method of reaching deep water. In addition, the crevices between the granite blocks offer cover to many small creatures such as sticklebacks and loaches, and well the trout know that fact.

The granite blocks today are wet with spray, so off come the waders. The wind is much stronger here than it was in the corner sheltered by the land, and 18yd will be our longest cast, a longer line would soon be drowned. With the dam rising at the back, and the wind blowing almost straight in, we compromise by casting as shown in Diagram 1. Casting 18yd of line at 40° to the dam, our flies drop 11½yd from the margin, and are over 12ft to 16ft of water, depending on the slope of the dam. The second and third casts are made at 30° and 20° respectively. The last cast does not fish much new water, but it takes a lot of fish, namely: those that followed-in the first two casts. Of course it doesn't matter a jot if you cast at 42°, 28°, and 20°. But it is essential to realize that the angle or gap between each cast must bear some relationship to the size of the trout's window at the depth he is lying.

The relationship between the width of the window and the depth at which the fish is lying is approximately as 7 is to 4.

In 12ft of water the window would be 21ft across, and theoretically speaking, provided the casts were never wider apart than 21ft all fish within reach of the caster must see the fly at least once, while they continue to lie at 12ft depth.

But if the fish lie at 6ft and their window is narrowed to 10ft 6in, then casts separated by a distance of 21ft may escape the fishes' vision altogether. But please do not conclude that a fish can only see objects in his window, he can and often does see a fly which is a long way outside it. Under conditions of poor light, however, he will undoubtedly see the fly in the window more distinctly.

Even here on the dam the wind is causing a deep belly in the line, and we put the rod tip down to the water; for drag is so severe that the large fly is racing across the top. As the line comes round to the side we begin the lift, and the fly leaves the water not 2ft from the edge. By reaching well forward when we begin the pick-up we throw our line high at the back. By the way, never drop recovered line when you are fishing-out a cast or you will tread on it 'sure as eggs'. This mishap and the resultant cut line occur far too frequently to make the advice unnecessary.

Have you noticed yet that although your line leads straight away from you, the fly as you pick up seems to leave the water away over to the left? If you will glance back to Diagram 1 you will see what is

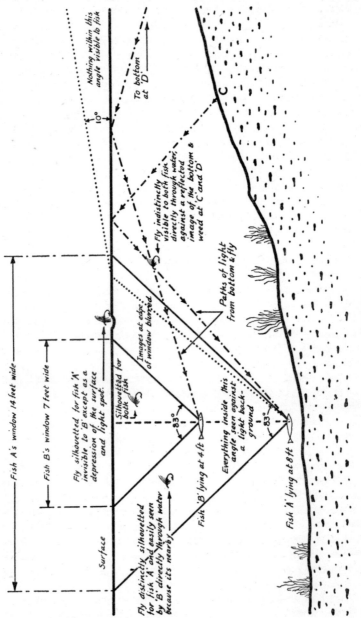

Nothing within this angle visible to fish

10°

To bottom at 'D'

C

Fly indistinctly visible to both fish directly through water, against a reflected image of the bottom & weed at 'C and 'D'

Paths of light from bottom & fly

Images at edge of window blurred

Fish A's window 14 feet wide

Fish B's window 7 feet wide

Fly silhouetted for fish 'A' invisible to 'B' except as a depression of the surface and light spot.

Silhouetted for both fish

83°

83°

Everything inside this angle seen against a light back-ground

Fish 'B' lying at 4 ft

Fish 'A' lying at 8 ft

Surface

Fly distinctly silhouetted for fish 'A' and easily seen by 'B' directly through water because its nearby

Diagram 3

happening. The thick line shows the position on casting. As you recover, your line bellies, until it lies as shown by the dotted line in the diagram.

All this means that it is no use looking down your line for the expected rise, for it is going to occur over to the left where the fly is. Try to imagine the path of your fly and keep your eyes fixed on the general area of water where this analysis tells you the fly is fishing.

After fishing out the three casts move down two paces; repeat the 'performance' *ad infinitum*. So short a move ensures that a fish sees the fly at least twice. Fine! I am going to fish down 30yd behind you.

'When does something happen?' you ask.

'Perhaps now, perhaps in two hours' time, perhaps no . . . but anyway, keep your mind on the job.'

Forty minutes later we are some 80yd farther down the dam and gloom reigns supreme. Conversation regarding lunch reveals a state of mind which is not conducive to good fishing. Just as you turn to speak, there is a wild commotion at the surface *not 3yd from the side* and you are into the first fish. Luckily he is only about 1¼lb or there would have been a break 'on the take'. As you play him, boredom quite gone, I notice the pressure of the wind on your rod is giving trouble. Under these conditions I often find that when the wind gusts I lose the 'feel' of the fish altogether: another argument for strong casts. Your large net makes child's play of the netting and having killed your fish which actually weighed 1lb 6oz you ask yourself whether or not to carry on down the dam.

In your position I would stay put. Possibly because the remains of old weed beds provide feed for tubifex, snail and nymph, the fish appear to be very localized along the dam, particularly in the early season. Having picked up one fish I would 'flog' 10yd either side of the spot for at least forty minutes before moving on down. I am aware that river etiquette demands that you move down, but we normally invite the chap behind to go in front. He will not mind provided you indicate to him what you intend to do. This sort of thing is the logical result of the fact that our fish behave differently from river fish.

You're going to fish it out? Splendid! I will go below you and look for a lie of my own.

Half an hour later, the wind has veered so as to blow straight into the dam at 20mph to 25mph. Ordinary 'flashers' have become useless – too light to stay submerged, and I have been using a 'Jersey Herd' for the last twenty minutes. So bad is the lop that I completely failed to see a rise, and became aware of it only as the line tightened. Before I could hit the fish he was gone. I have to admit to myself, I would probably have had him if I had been fully alert.

It having become almost impossible to control the 10yd of line to which we have been reduced, we decide to move.

The marginal shallows will normally fail to yield so well as the deep water, early on, particularly in a cold spring. However, it is still only 11.30, and from now to 1pm should be the best part of the day so we will move up the far bank to the point of the bay.

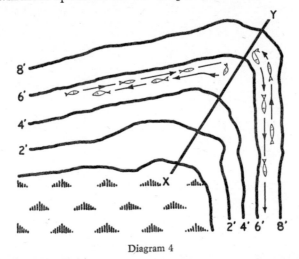

Diagram 4

Trout usually cruise along a certain depth-line. Having reached a position such as that represented by the line XY in the above diagram of a typical point, the fish find the water deepening and turn around. Thus from the point we are able to fish to two groups of fish.

We enter the water slowly, making as little disturbance as possible, casting ahead of us in case there is a fish lying close in.

We commence fishing about 20yd apart: in these water conditions two lines close together will not worry the fish. By the way, an approach to 30yd from another angler is seldom resented provided you wade very quietly and do not cast to fish which he can reach and is in fact fishing for. Often enough, if he is unable to cast when a fish rises within his distance, he will invite you to 'put over him quickly', and you are expected to 'have a go'. Ours is friendly fishing.

Since the wind is behind my right shoulder, and the line is tending to blow down on me, I don a pair of goggles. I used to cast over my left shoulder, but it restricted my power, and therefore my distance.

Few anglers bother to change their casting shoulder under such conditions, most of us, myself included, are well able to throw the line clear. But it must be faced that in severe winds no one has full control of his line, and anything can happen.

Because of the danger to the eyes it is always advisable to keep well to the back when passing behind someone fishing and shout 'Passing' and 'Clear' in case he has not seen you.

After fishing for some fifteen minutes, I hear what may have been a rise some 25yd away, so I move up and cover the area. I continue fishing fast to keep in touch with the fly, and fish as deep as I can, and after some twenty minutes have a heavy pull; only the rod well over as in Diagram 2 saves me from a break. There was no warning swirl, just a pull which was in fact the start of the first rush and I have not driven home the hook yet. Despite the heavy take, a number of fish are lost if you neglect to tighten hard as soon as the rush slackens, so, with rod high, at arm's length, I make sure of the hook-hold. Striking twice is no advantage, in fact, you may loosen a secure hold.

The fight is a fast one and pace soon slackens. I unclip the net and rest it in front of me. Two minutes later the fish is brought within reach; it rolls, for a moment off balance – the fight is over. I put on strain – never mess about with fish at this stage – slide him head on the surface towards me with net ready, submerged, and lift without haste as he comes over it. On the balance he goes 3lb 2oz, in two month's time he would be 6oz heavier, but nevertheless he is in reasonably good condition.

Some twenty minutes later I receive another pull but do not connect. A further twenty minutes yields nothing, and, it being 1.15pm, we leave the water and have lunch. Two fish by lunch is good going at this time of year.

Sandwiches gone, we move up to the top-end. The walk warms us up, but apart from that gives us little satisfaction, for no fish are moving. The afternoon is seldom a good period, but it is too cold to sit about and we came to fish after all. It is only about 4ft deep up here, and we may come across some of the four-year-old well-mended fish which will already be feeding on nymph: even in this cold weather small hatches of fly do take place and many nymphs are active. After fishing for half an hour using Black and Peacock Spider and Brown Nymph (at the up-wind end of the reservoir the water is much calmer and the wind less troublesome, making it possible to fish slowly) we both hook fish within a matter of seconds of one another. They fight, weight for weight, far better than the three-pounder and both weigh 1lb 3oz. Obviously several fish moved by us and will probably return, so without wasting time we get back to work.

One and a half hours later, having paused only to change flies – an effective means of ensuring that you are not fishing with a cast which has 'hinged' at the fly – we have had no further offer and decide that a spot of something warm is indicated. The wind by now has moderated and veered, the air is slightly warmer and it begins to rain.

Thermos flasks emptied, we move back to the dam and find that the wind is blowing along it, having veered through 130° since the forenoon.

Fishing hard, with 'flashers' of sizes 8 and 9 to keep down – line-drag is tending to 'race' the flies across the top again – we move along the dam, casting as in the morning but working from the opposite end of the dam. Fading light finds us with no more fish and we pack up. We have made the most of our opportunities and have a brace apiece for our efforts. What of the others?

One angler has taken two fish from the dam: he apparently fished hard there after we had given it up as hopeless, and took both fish just where we took our first. The others are blank, having fished where it was comfortable to cast rather than where the fish were likely to be.

Had it been a warm, spring day, with the water temperature customary in mid-May, we would have fished much as we would for that time of year, except that we would have concentrated on the deep water and fished our flies deep if the fish were not on top.

Many anglers consider the early season fishing as time wasted. It is true that big bags are seldom made, but on the other hand you are getting in practice, and when the good fishing does come you are in trim to make the most of it.

We fishermen can find excuses for every kind of madness we indulge in.

CHAPTER EIGHT

The Cream of the Season's Sport

WERE I ASKED WHAT PART OF THE SEASON gave limit bags most frequently, I would unhesitatingly reply, 'mid-May to mid-June'. Yet, when I look at my records I find that in some years the period in question has been quite poor: 1950 saw excellent sport – sixteen fish in my ten outings from 11 May to 10 June; in a season when top score was thirty-five fish; 1949, on the other hand, was one of the bad years mentioned above – only eight fish in my twelve outings from 7 May to 25 June. My diary entry for Wednesday, 25 May, reads as follows:

'Fished from 9am to 9pm Wind W force 4 to 5 (Beaufort Scale). Cold. Leaden Sky. Six anglers on water: all blank. No fish have been taken on this water for fourteen days.'

It was during this period that I took but one fish in five outings. While on this dismal topic of blanks, I feel it might be some encouragement to the reservoir novice 'enjoying' a sticky period to read that I once had a period of twelve outings with only one fish. Reservoir fishing is something you have to stick at and master. One should never 'write off' a water after only three or four blank visits. Men who know the water still have blanks and many of them. I feel the newcomer should be prepared to make six visits before becoming downhearted about his lack of *luck*.

If you find that you will be able to fish twice during a given week, I most strongly suggest that you fish on two consecutive days if possible. On the second day you will be able to exploit with advantage what you learned on the previous day. On the other hand, to fish, say on the Monday and again on the Friday, means that on the Friday you will have a completely different set of problems to solve, for a change of wind and weather will have altered the whole picture.

It is in May that we begin to feel that we are truly fly-fishing. Hatches of the natural take place almost every day and the fish readily take near the surface.

Of course, in some years, 1951 was an example, prolonged cold weather persisting into early June causes the whole pattern of behaviour of the fish to go 'haywire'. To be strictly accurate, the cycle remains much the same but local migrations occur later or earlier depending on water temperature, weed growth and other natural phenomena.

The cold northerly winds which plagued us on our last visit to the water at 'Floganper Spire' are changed to light south-westerly breezes; rushes are springing up along the margins, and the water-weed is beginning to show beneath the surface in the shallows. The air, too, is warm, and one is filled with a sense of Nature's exuberant activity. Today, we ought to be able to see the fish move and it will be well worth our while to look for rising fish.

As we tackle-up at the boathouse, a keen watch on the water reveals several rises on the edge of the ripple a hundred yards or so up the bank. We shall not fish deep water today, for by now the majority of the fish are feeding in the marginal shallows. The water is very clear – its usual state in calm weather – and we decide to use 11ft casts, with heavy butts tapering to ·010in. Too heavy, you think? Perhaps, but then it must be remembered that ·010in nylon is no more visible than ·009in gut, and it is best to fish as heavy as conditions will allow.

Today is a 'Black and Peacock Spider' day, and size 7 will do nicely to start with.

We make our way along the bank and find the fish still moving. The rises are taking place over a distance of 35yd along the edge of the ripple, and an occasional 'hump' or swirl in the calm water 20yd from the shore reveals the presence of at least one other fish nymphing hard.

After watching carefully for several moments we notice that the rises occur in definite sequence: one up on the left, followed by one in front, then another a little to our right, and then the order is reversed. The rises follow one another quickly and it is hard to realize that they are made by one fish moving fast. The nearer nymphing fish will be the easier to take, and in any case it would be folly to cast across them in order to take the more distant fish.

We enter the water a few feet and hold the fly under water, squeezing it to expel air from the body and ensure its ready sinking. Without moving any farther from the shore and ignoring the individual swirls, we begin dropping our fly just short of the area of activity. There is no point in fanning the casts: we are fishing in water the fish are using.

We have slowly increased our length of line and the fly is now dropping well inside the target area. As we lift the rod point and take the line in the left hand preparatory to recovering line, we are taken heavily and broken. A bad start! It happens now and again and we just have to face it: there must always be a brief instant after delivering the fly when the line and rod are not fully controlled.

Somewhat shakily we tie on another 'Spider', and having soaked it, again cover the same spot, recovering line slowly to avoid 'wake'. The fly is fishing only about 15in below the surface for, as frequently happens in calm water, the upper 3ft of the cast is refusing to submerge. After half a dozen casts we are taken. There is no 'tighten' because of the slack line between rod-tip and water, but the cast is suddenly seen to 'disappear through a hole in the water'. I am not being facetious, that is exactly what appears to happen. We drive home the barb smoothly and easily by raising the whole rod. This 'turn of the wrist' business, presumably a sort of roach strike, gives a very high percentage of breaks.

What a difference in the strength of the fish since opening day. Warmer water has speeded up the rate of conversion of food into energy and flesh, and the fish are much stronger. In no time our backing line is disappearing. The rod held high exerts little strain on the fish, but towing an increasingly long line will stop him eventually. The line is leading directly away from us, and we are somewhat surprised when the fish suddenly jumps once, twice . . . six times in all, about 50yd out; but away over to the right. He loses much of his steam after this effort, and although we cannot feel the fish, line comes in easily enough. Thankfully, we see the splice pass down the rings, and a few seconds later we see the fish swimming across our front just beneath the surface and 10yd away. The net is quietly unshipped, and then he sees us and is off again at tremendous speed straight into a weed bed on the left.

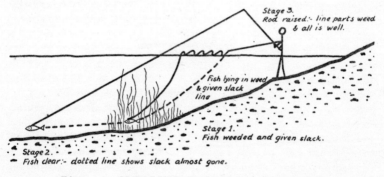

Diagram 1 CLEARING FISH FROM WEED BED

Satisfied that he is still on, we put down the rod point and pull steadily on the line. No luck: he's in the thick of it. We pull off a few yards of line; leave it slack on the water and wait. About five minutes later the slack commences to move, and we strip off a few more yards. Just before it is all gone, we raise the rod and arm above the head and tighten on the fish once more. He is now on the far side of the weed bed and the tight line parts the weed and all is well again.

This method works for me in nine out of ten cases: it is very seldom a fish is lost.

Again we bring the very tired fish close in, but he is still on balance and we must be prepared for more 'fun and games'. Yes, I thought so. He makes a sudden rush and we see the cast begin to lengthen: he's coming out. Quickly we lower the rod-tip sideways and down to the water; he turns down leaving only a swirl where might have been a smother of spray followed by catastrophe when the hook-hold gave. A few moments later he is led to the net and we administer last rites. Three pounds twelve ounces he goes: a beautifully-conditioned fish. We open his mouth and find it full of the inevitable olive nymphs.

Perhaps you wonder why we took no steps to lower the rod when he jumped after that first rush. The reason was that there was no point in doing so. By far the greatest strain on the cast was caused by the long length of submerged line which was being towed. Slack line at the rod end would have made no difference whatsoever if the fish had fallen back on the cast. If you find that fish go into a succession of wild gymnastics in the first few seconds you are probably holding them too hard, although it sometimes betokens a light hook-hold.

We wade back into the water to tackle the surface-feeding fish: he is still rising despite all the commotion.

He rises some 15yd on the left moving our way, so we cast to the edge of the ripple some 5yd to our right: it pays to make sure of being ahead. We recover line slowly and see his shoulder break water 3yd to the left of the fly and almost immediately afterwards he rises again to the right of the fly. A refusal? Perhaps, but that shoulder rise indicated that he was moving very near the surface and possibly he passed over the fly and is only interested in what appears in his window. Here is a case for greasing the cast down to the last 18in, so that the fly fishes only about 3in below the surface. A size 5 fly will be plenty big enough. Again we cast well ahead of him and several moments later he takes while moving fast; feels the point immediately, and shoots clean out of the water. The rod takes the shock nicely and he is played out without incident, and inspected on shore. He is markedly a different fish from our first. He is thicker for his length, silvery like a sea-trout and black spotted. He is obviously of a different race of fish. Only occasionally do we take fish of this type, and more often than not they are surface-feeding at the time they are caught.

I believe that Edward Hewitt's plankton theory supplies the answer for the existence of these fish.

Undoubtedly, some of our fish are wild-bred, and in the fry stage would be plankton feeders, a habit which Hewitt tells us artificially fed hatchery-fish probably fail to acquire. It is possible that fry-stocking might result in more surface-feeding fish since a fly does represent a good mouthful to a small fish in the wild state, and the habit once acquired would persist.

But what of our fishing? There is no more activity that we can see – there probably are several more fish feeding down below – but today we shall cast to rising fish while they are to be found.

We walk about half a mile along the shore and see nothing so we decide to return to our old spot. There too the surface is undisturbed and a change of tactics is indicated. Off comes the cast and in its place we tie on a cast of at least 12ft length with a dropper 6ft above the point. On the dropper we tie a Brown Nymph, while as tail fly we use a leaded Black and Peacock Spider. Had we not taken a fish earlier on the 'Spider' we should probably have used a green nymph. We none of us care to change a winning team!

The whole of our present tactics is based on the fact that we do not know at what depth fish are feeding, and we therefore propose to fish at two depths.

The cast is soaped to facilitate its sinking, and having moved 20yd away from that weed bed we commence casting. The flies are allowed to sink deep before we begin to recover line, in fact the tail fly should be allowed to sink to the bottom, when the 'pull and pause' recovery recommended for the Green Nymph will cause disturbance of the mud, and attract the attention of fish. The dropper is fishing some 2ft to 3ft above the bottom and is thus serving a real purpose. After casting for half an hour, the line is drawn sharply and we tighten into our third fish, and presently land him.

This method will usually pay-off at this time of year, but it does require enormous concentration.

Still nothing showing anywhere! This seems as good an opportunity for eating as is likely to occur today. We have taken three fish; all is well with the world, and we decide to take a nap rather than risk catching our fourth and last fish too early in the day.

This is an excellent way of missing a 'limit'!

Friend, if you want a limit – and we all do now and again – then you must catch it while you may, in an hour's time it may be too late.

Nevertheless, on this occasion we decide 'things are different'. 'This is the time of year when fish feed all day,' we tell ourselves.

At three o'clock we awaken, and picking up our rod and net wade confidently into the water to catch that last fish. With luck we shall be home in time for tea, and come what may we shall certainly be home early enough to take our wife to see a film.

By four o'clock we are resigned to missing tea. By five o'clock we have walked round to the other side of the water to cover some 'easier' fish: fish that have not been 'flogged' all day.

By six o'clock, our wife has missed her outing to the pictures; that limit is as far away as ever, and we are fishing in deadly earnest.

Twenty minutes before we are due back at the boat house to weigh-in, a fool of a fish, the first we have seen since the morning, rises 20yd on our left at the edge of a weed bed.

Despairingly we throw a nymph at him; and miraculously he takes.

'It is too much of a "gift" to be so easy,' you tell yourself, and are very relieved when the fish is safely netted.

Of course you were never really in doubt as to your ability to get that fourth fish, but it's too bad it had to come so late in the day. You know perfectly well that wives won't believe a word about the outing to the pictures, and on the whole it would be better not to mention it.

On arrival home you will be accused of having a good day out without so much as a thought for your wife or children.

Life is very hard!

To return however to the matter of the day's sport. We recall that the three fish taken before lunch were taken in flat calm water. Water which many anglers avoid, yet, like most problems in fishing, there was an answer requiring only a little thought.

CHAPTER NINE

High Summer

MID-JULY TO MID-AUGUST is, for many of us, a heart-breaking period. From dawn to sunset the sun beats down mercilessly out of a clear sky on to the mirror-like surface of the reservoir, the water of which, needless to say, is crystal clear. Well, maybe! It is more probable of course that it will be dull with occasional showers, and blowing half a gale to boot. Whatever the weather, we must not blame it too much: it is not the primary cause of small bags. The worst enemy is weed, and only slightly less damnable is the attitude of the fish. Gone are the days of heavy feeding, the fish are now in condition and do not need to feed continuously as they did in May. In addition, the ova is by now well developed, and is beginning to cause the fish some discomfort.

In an average year the water will have dropped some 7ft by mid-July, and the bottom over which we took fish earlier in the year will by now be dry land. Extending to some 30yd from the margin and seemingly continuing in an unbroken stretch right round the water is the weed. Do not let it scare you: it is nowhere nearly so dense as it appears at first sight. Move round the water and you will find open bays in the weed, and in other places you will be able to wade out far enough to reach the open water beyond it.

Like the fisherman, the trout prefers open water, and you can be quite certain that if you fish these bays you will be covering trout, which is 90 per cent of the battle. If you find fish rising, then fish for them with a size 5 or 6 Black and Peacock Spider or Brown Nymph. Remember to grease your cast for there may be weed 12in below the surface. If you catch-up on weed as you recover line and the fish still rises, put on a big fuzzy-buzzy dry-fly and cast so as to lay the nylon across the weed, with the fly 6in from the edge, in open water. Allow it to sit there until you are quite certain the fish has passed it and refused, or until you become bored.

This is not the only approach to dry-fly angling which the reservoir affords, but it is the approach which is most commonly used. Strangely enough it can be quite effective and I have taken several fish doing it: fish which would not look at a wet-fly. It could well be that these fish were taken because they saw nothing of the line.

59

Ernest Phillips in a letter to *Fishing Gazette* on 1 December 1951, wrote of a 'school' of dry-fly men who fished a reservoir presumably near to his home, Doncaster. He described how these anglers cast out their flies and sat down to await results, which deservedly were slow to come, for trout abhor lines: they kept out of range of those 'telegraph poles' lying across an otherwise unbroken surface.

I have seen this method in use many times, often enough while the fisherman is eating his sandwiches. Occasionally a fish is taken, and it is surprising how proud the captor becomes of his success fishing 'dry', though what he has done to earn his fish it is hard to say.

Naturally this is not the method used by men such as E.K. who study dry-fly tactics in much the same way that I study the wet-fly. They present a fly to a rising fish when possible, or cast their dry-fly around the edges of weed beds and work the fly very much as a wet-fly is worked. Certainly they get fish, but few of them would claim that they take anywhere near so many fish as the wet-fly man.

One of my severest critics, an enthusiastic reservoir dry-fly fisherman, writing in *Fishing Gazette*, stated 'It is evident Mr Ivens is a wet-fly man, by which means I agree more fish are taken out of still water.' Those words sum up my case. When the top score for a water is only thirty-five fish, and when those thirty-five fish represent twenty-seven days' hard fishing with a wet-fly, then the further handicap which the dry-fly places upon the angler is quite unwarranted. Where fish are easy to take the whole situation is changed and a 'dry-fly only' rule might be reasonable.

A few moments ago I referred to dry-fly fishing as a luncheon interlude, and it brought to my mind a striking case of the operation of the long arm of coincidence.

During a sweltering July morning of 1950, three of us, old friends, foregathered for lunch at the bridge-hole on a nearby water. The reservoir is divided into two parts by a dam carrying a public roadway. The apparently separated stretches of water are connected by means of a bridge under the roadway.

The bridge-hole, like all bridge-holes, has a good reputation as a holding spot and there are many stories connected with it.

As we ate, Jim recalled how, many years before, an angler had sat where we were, his fly dangling in the water below his feet. The inevitable happened, a trout took the fly; and rod, reel and line were pulled into the water.

Now all three of us had fished the 'hole' at varying times during

Plate XIX

Sometimes the fish are in the surf on the lee-shore. Under these conditions short-lining is the only method worth while. (*See page 62*)

Plate XX

'High Summer'. Many fishermen take one look at the heavily weeded margins and pass them over as unfishable, but bays like this one are always to be found, and the man who fishes them in July will often kill the only fish of the day. (*See page* 59)

Durleigh is the supply reservoir of Bridgwater, Somerset, and is well stocked with hard fighting trout of large size. Fine tackle is quite out of place in this water.

t.he morning and not one of us had seen a fish. On hearing the story,
my second companion unhitched his fly from the cork of the butt and
dropped it into the water. We carried on eating.

Some ten minutes later a light breeze through the bridge lifted the
line, and immediately an explosion in the water announced a 'take'.
My friend grabbed at his rod, the trout – a fish of at least 4lb – bolted
through the bridge and broke the cast.

That was the only fish anyone moved that day!

To my certain knowledge the original story was true, and a like
incident had never occurred until it was repeated in the presence of
two witnesses.

Fishing is full of such surprises.

In these July days few rising fish will be seen after 10am, and with
no fish showing and in brilliant light the best method is 'short-
lining'.

Find a stretch of the weed with pockets leading to open water or
alternatively a stretch where you can wade to within 8yd of the edge
of the weed and cast beyond and along the edge. Use a point of at
least ·010in and a leaded Alexandra of size 7 or 8. Using a maximum
of 15yd of line, drop your fly in open water; allow it to sink about
15in and take the line *lightly* between thumb and forefinger below the
first ring. Draw the line evenly by carrying the left hand away to the
left side of the body, at the same time slowly raising the rod tip as
though you were making a very slow pick-up. When the left arm is
almost fully extended and the rod is at half past eleven, the rod is
accelerated and the fly leaves the water. The spare line is shot out on
the forward punch. The line should travel well to the side and low,
on the lift, and overhead on the forward punch. The cast is very
similar to the downward-cut cast for shooting into wind, except that
the low punch is not required. The essential is a continuous motion.
The line length remains constant. You deliver the fly; pause; pull
with left hand and lift off and throw back; throw forward and shoot
to re-deliver the fly. Each time the fly drops in a different spot and
you search every inch of the open water, particularly the edges of the
weed, with a very fast-moving 'flasher'. Fully 50 per cent of takes occur
as you lift off, so again, never hold the line tightly. Move fast and
cover a lot of water.

As an alternative to the Alexandra, you might find it profitable to
use a 'Jersey Herd' until you are followed and then, having found a
fish, try for him with a nymph as outlined in Chapter 6.

Fish taken while 'short-lining' are usually big cannibals, and land-
ing them is a problem. Funnily enough, most fish make for open
water. I tire them, away out, whenever I can, and then when they
quieten off I apply pressure and bring them straight to the net. If I

am weeded, I merely give them slack and proceed as mentioned in my last chapter. More than once I have skidded a fish across the top of a weed bed, on his tail. It is a dangerous thing to do at any time, but with a tip-actioned rod it would be downright silly.

Since we have mentioned the short-line method of fishing, I would like to deal with its further application.

Fish tend to move into the wind and it usually pays to fish the up-wind side of the water. But when the wind is strong and waves beat upon the lee-shore the water there becomes very coloured and fish will be found feeding on the creatures stirred from the bottom by the action of the water. Use an 8ft steep-tapered cast and a Black and Peacock Spider: black is far more easily seen by the fish in murky water than is any other colour. Assuming that you have a few yards of open water close in at the side, wade well out and move along, dropping the fly about 2yd from the margin, casting and lifting as mentioned above. It is surprising how close the fish are to the shore in rough water. Fight down your disbelief, and remember that bass fishermen often take good fish by casting their tackle into the surf, where the bass are feeding on creatures washed off the bottom by the breakers. I scarcely dare to mention it, but you can create murky water in calm weather by wading backwards, doing a Charleston as you go. You short-line the water you have waded. I have done this twice and have taken fish on both occasions, but it is not very sporting and may lead to bother with the water-authorities who require minimum sediment to avoid silting up filter-beds.

The short-line method, used with a downward cut cast, is very useful for fishing into a strong wind.

Sometimes, having found fish feeding well at the surface on the upwind shore, you arrive on the water on the following day to find the wind has veered through 180° and is blowing off the opposite shore.

As I have said, I like to fish the upwind shore, but now and again, and usually immediately following a sudden change in the wind such as that just mentioned, fishing the upwind shore just fails to give the results.

The answer usually lies in the fact that the fish have not yet adjusted themselves to the change in the wind. After all, the surface drift in the new wind direction takes some little time to develop, and until it develops and the instinct of the fish to head into the current is triggered-off, there is little reason for the fish to move over to the 'new' upwind shore.

I do not believe that creatures blown on to the water from the upwind shore have much to do with this upwind migration, for surface food has little attraction for the vast majority of our fish. The surface current shown in the diagram is more likely to be the cause of migration.

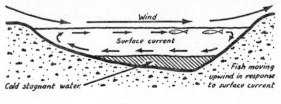

Diagram 1

Perhaps the most striking illustration in my experience of this tendency to delay migration for some time after a change in wind direction occurred on 22 May 1948. On the previous day I had taken a limit in shallow water at the narrow, upper end of the reservoir, the wind being east-north-east. On the morning of the 22nd the wind was west-north-west and I fished from 9am to 11am at a point immediately opposite the spot I had fished on the previous day, without an offer. I moved round to my old spot and within thirty minutes had my limit, short-lining both the margin and the open water. Of course, it was my birthday! To sum up: we may assume that for several hours after a change of wind-direction the fish will remain at their old spot.

These uses of the short line are not confined to high summer, they can be applied at any time in the season. And now to our friend the 'sticklebacker'.

This 'thug' appears when the fry are seen as patches of black needles on the surface of the water near the dam and round the weed-beds. The fry appear in their millions about the middle of July and the fish go mad in an orgy of feastings.

When the fish first become aware, as it were, of this new food-form, their attack is somewhat haphazard; but later it has all the markings of a planned military operation. The fish cruise slowly behind the shoal of fry shepherding it towards the dam or into a bay in the weed. Suddenly you see the fry begin to skitter along the surface; a furrow appears behind the fry, and then the water is broken by a series of slashing sallies on the part of the trout as he takes his toll. I have heard it alleged that the fish dashes in with his mouth wide open, but though I have watched a trout do it hundreds of times, often at a distance of only 6ft, I still have not been able to see just how he takes. He moves like lightning on roller-skates and can only just be seen through the flurry of spray he throws up. It is the most exciting thing in fishing.

For the first week of the sticklebacking season the trout are easy to take, but it is no use casting continuously. Spot your fish; check up on his beat and lay your line out on the water well away from the fish. As soon as you see the fry skitter at the surface, pick up line and throw ahead of them and across their path if possible; recover line slowly. Usually you will be taken within three seconds, but if the fish ignores you, keep drawing: he may take you as he turns away from the shoal when your fly will be the only moving object in sight. I usually find the Black and Peacock Spider ideal for this fishing, as it fishes high in the water. However, if you are refused several times, change to a big fly, an Alexandra or a Green and Brown Nymph, and fish it fast across his nose as he furrows the water. If he still refuses – give up. You are fishing for a laddie who knows all the answers. I shall deal with these fish in my next chapter, but since in the early part of this form of feeding the feeding period may last only thirty minutes, you have no time to waste and should look for another fish. Late in August many fish feed on stickleback for the whole day, and then you will have time to plan a campaign.

Remember then, that this is one occasion when a single well-placed and well-timed cast will do more good than two hours' flogging. Provided that the fish have not fed hard all day, there should be good fishing in the evening rise. You may have day time and evening feeding of course; but it is unlikely.

Taken by and large, the dam is usually as productive as any spot in the evening. Often it is the only place where fish rise within reach. I always dry and grease my line about 6pm; nothing is more infuriating than to have one's line sink just as the rise starts. You will find that if you strip your casting line off your reel and allow it to dry, whenever you sit down for a few moments, line-sinking will trouble you much less. If you have line-sinking trouble owing to 'water-bloom', the algal scum often present on reservoirs particularly when barometric pressures are low, there is no real cure but to move to a part of the water which is clear of this nuisance.

It is essential that the line should be wiped down with a clean soft cloth after contact with an algal scum. Greasing will not otherwise be successful.

The method of fishing the evening rise is quite simple. Using a size 6 Black and Peacock Spider or any other wet-fly which will fish high in the water, cast to the rising fish exactly as though you were presenting a dry-fly, and draw slowly. If you have no success, you must assume the fish are moving fast and that you are not covering them quickly enough. Your best method, then, is to ignore the rises and fish slowly through the area of activity. If you still remain fishless, change to a size 4 fly; cast; let it sink, and watch your cast carefully. Very often fish which refuse a horizontally-moving fly will readily seize a sinking one. This behaviour is not confined to the evening rise, but occurs more often then. The take, as I have said before, may appear as a straightening of the cast, or the disappearance of the cast 'through a hole in the water'.

Fish which 'head and tail' are hard to hit, largely because we train ourselves to tighten the moment we see, feel, hear or sense anything happening. The head and tailer takes on the way down and we usually strike as he breaks water, which is much too soon.

I hope I have shown you that July days are not impossible, though, of course, very high temperatures sicken the fish. When the water is unpleasantly warm, you will do best to concentrate upon the periods before 10am and after 8pm: sport is unlikely in the heat of the noon and afternoon sun, although you may take fish very deep down in a cooler layer of water.

CHAPTER TEN

Late August and the Back-End

FOR THE LAST TWO WEEKS OF AUGUST and possibly for the first two weeks of September as well, the sticklebacker will provide most of the sport. Few other fish move during the day, and the sticklebacker makes his presence so obvious that it is not surprising that most of these fish are 'flogged' very heavily.

By the time the trout have been feeding on fry for a fortnight most of them know that there is an unpleasant connection between the man on the bank and the line which drops on the water. Having recognized the connection, the fish continue to feed as though the angler and his gear were not there at all. Their heavy feeding among the fry continues unabated, often within feet of the angler, but they very seldom make a mistake and take the fly. It is essential that the angler recognize when he is up against an 'educated' fish, and change his tactics before too much time has been lost. If I may generalize again, I would say that any sticklebacker which has its beat in a frequently-fished position requires special treatment, as does also any fish which has refused a well-presented fly three times.

I had an excellent example of the futility of fishing for these 'wide boys' by orthodox methods on 24 September 1949. The fish were mad-on from 9am to 6pm. There must have been forty fish working the shoals of fry along the first 200yd of the dam, and all six of us flogged these fish until we were reduced to incoherent, impotent rage. At about 2pm, I moved away from the others, and threw at a solitary fish down by the valve tower. Three times I cast; three times he rose, and three times I missed him. That fish was the first that anyone had risen that day. I sat down for a moment to smoke a cigarette, calm down and think things over. I was a full 20yd from the fish when I rose it, and I was certain that no one else had fished for it that day; perhaps that was the answer.

I moved on down to the shallow bay at the far end of the dam, and immediately noticed several fish working the fry not more than 5yd from the margin. I knelt down well back from the water and waited for a fish to move towards me. To cut a short story shorter, in twenty minutes I made three casts, and took three fish. I was then joined by two other anglers who, seeing the fish still feeding confidently, flogged away at them. The fish were not at all put out by lines and flies flopping all over the place: they continued operations among the fry; but none of them made a mistake from that moment. I left the water early, but so far as I know, no other fish were taken that day. I learnt later that the sticklebackers 'went down' at about 6pm, and as was only to be expected after such heavy daytime feeding, there was no evening rise despite a quantity of fly on the water.

Whenever I find myself up against an 'educated' fish, I follow certain definite tactics based on two fundamental necessities. Firstly, the fish must never see me until he is hooked; and secondly, he must see the fly before he sees the cast or line.

Before fishing, I watch the fish carefully to find the limits of his beat. If he is more than 10yd from the shore, I wade out; place myself 20yd from the end of his beat, and wait for him to work towards me. I usually use a Brown and Green Nymph, size 7 or 8 (remember its minnowish appearance?) for this work, and drop it *well* ahead of the fish and along the line of his beat. I draw slowly until he either takes or passes it. If the latter, I continue drawing until I can pick up the line with no possibility of the fish being near to the inevitable slight disturbance of the surface which occurs on picking up.

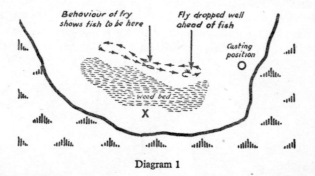

Diagram 1

This diagram shows the beat of a typical sticklebacker, and my probable approach to a fish in such a position. Unless it is quite impossible to fish the ends of the beat, I never cast across the line of advance of the fish. All too often when I do cast from a position such as X in the diagram, the cast drops very near to the fish, and the chance of taking him after such treatment is almost nil. True, there is always a daft 'un.

On several occasions, having failed with a large Green and Brown Nymph, I have changed to a size 4 Brown Nymph and taken the fish first cast. Which again argues the pointlessness of the exact or close imitation. To further bewilder the reader as to what goes on in the minds of these fish of ours, I must in fairness record the fact that E.K.

67

takes a number of difficult fish each year by floating a dry-fly on their beat, and often enough fish taken in this way are very large.

Surely, if ever proof were needed of the fact that fish will take anything which might be food once the urge to feed is upon them, this proof is supplied by the 5lb trout which having fed for hours on fry, suddenly dashes at a Coch-y-bondhu and seizes it.

Nevertheless, these occurrences are exceptions and E.K.'s success must not persuade you that the method is anything but a last resort to be used when all other methods have failed.

During late August and September, the Silverhorn Fly appears in great numbers. My knowledge of entomology is strictly limited, I cannot even guess at the genus and species of the insect, but if I describe it as a small grey-brown sedge with antennae about ½in long, you will probably know what insect I refer to as a 'Silverhorn'. If this fly is going to appear on the water in the evening you will usually find them lying-up in the grasses during the daytime. At dusk, provided the wind is not more than 8mph to 10mph, they fly over the water; knot, and tumble on to the surface where the trout are waiting for them.

I know of no other fly which will cause the wild surface-activity, on the part of the fish, occasioned by the Silverhorn. I have seen a stretch of unbroken surface become a seething maelstrom in two

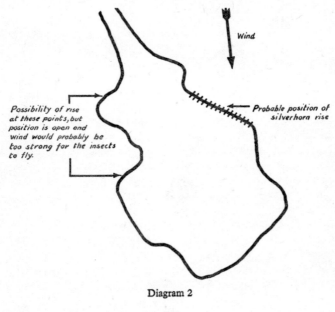

Diagram 2

minutes: where not one fish was to be seen hundreds appeared as the first flies fluttered across the surface. The rise is usually very localized. Perhaps 100yd of the marginal shallows will be boiling with fish while the remainder of the water continues undisturbed. Fortunately, it is possible to make a fairly accurate guess as to where it will take place.

The rise always occurs on the up-wind shore and usually at a point where the wind is blowing off and slightly along the shore as in Diagram 2.

In choosing your spot, you should remember that the wind usually drops to 'light airs' at dusk, and that the edge of the ripple which is within reach at 7pm may be 200yd away at 8.30pm. Where the wind blows 'off and along' the shore, the edge of the ripple should remain within reach. The edge of the ripple is very important for it is the point at which the wind strikes the water, and the flies are being carried by that wind.

Having found Silverhorn Fly in the grasses during the day, I spend the time after 7pm preparing for the evening rise. If several of us are fishing together, we spread out and watch the water over a 400yd stretch. When the rise starts, we all hasten to the spot and fish within yards of one another. When it is all over, we slowly and despondently wade ashore and try to think up a few new reasons for having failed to land a fish despite having had many 'offers'. Therein lies the point of this discourse: very few fish are taken during the fifteen to thirty crazy minutes which the rise usually occupies. I have an entry in front of me at this moment which records that from 8pm to 9pm on 16 August 1948, I rose, pricked and lost no fewer than eleven fish in addition to those which rose and failed to connect at all. I tried everything: rod point down, rod horizontal and at 90° to the line, striking at the rise, waiting for the pull . . . all to no purpose. A friend, fishing 'dry', fared no better: he rose fish but failed to connect. This type of experience is so common that I am toying with the idea that the fish are not feeding at all, but are merely 'sporting'. I believe they seize the fly and eject it. All the fish I have taken during the Silverhorn rise have been very lightly hooked at the front of the jaws and, more often than not, the fly has fallen out when the fish was in the net. However, it is great fun provided your mental stability is not in question, and you do sometimes pick up a brace of fish to compensate for other disappointments.

I have noticed that immediately the rise starts I often land a fish, and, again, during the period between the end of the rise and darkness, when all is quiet, I sometimes take a second fish. During the peak of the rise I merely miss fish galore.

The Black and Peacock Spider is far and away the best pattern, and size 5 is quite large enough. I usually fish 'greased-cast' so that the fly fishes shallow, and I see as much as possible of the take. I entirely ignore the individual rises (the fish are moving very fast and in no predictable direction) and merely cast and draw my fly through the area of activity.

I would not presume to advise further on tactics, for I have not yet developed a fully satisfactory method of fishing this rise. Stick to the Black and Peacock Spider, even if it does not produce a rise straight-way, and keep on fishing over the same water after the rise is over, sinking the cast so as to get the fly down deep. During these last few minutes you will be tired and probably mentally relaxed after the excitement of the rise. Keep your point up, it is almost certain to be a smash-take when it does come.

There is a tendency amongst anglers to fish larger flies because it is getting dark. I have experimented on this point and my conclusion is that it pays to continue using the same size of fly as was successful before darkness fell.

The last fortnight of the season sees the fish reverting to their sur-face-feeding habits of May and June. If you can get away from the work-bench or office during this period, you are almost certain to find good sport and perhaps a 'case fish', though being heavy with spawn the fight is a trial of strength rather than a thrilling, dashing affair.

And so we have been through the season on a typical Midland reservoir or lake. There must be dozens of 'stunt methods' which I have not mentioned at all, but the basic approach to most problems is there for you to build upon. In writing a work upon such a subject as fishing where every man differs in mental approach, technique, endurance and so on, only basic principles are of practical use.

CHAPTER ELEVEN

High Morale

WITH ALMOST NAUSEATING FREQUENCY we read that some politician, army officer or film star inspected the long-suffering men of such-and-such a regiment and came away much impressed by the obviously high morale of the men. It would be a piece of impertinence for me to suggest that the 'P.B. infantryman' would be only too pleased if various people worried less about his morale, but the fact is he would be delighted. On the other hand, he would also admit, reluctantly, that his morale is important to people like you and me.

Over the last few years the morale of the civilian population has also received its share of attention. Many hard-working, high-productivity operators in mines and factories have been persuaded to pose for photographs which have later appeared in various journals, thereby earning for the individual concerned the esteem of the general public and the disapproval of his fellow workers.

'Morale', it seems, is everything. I looked the word up in the 'Oxford Concise' and discovered two things about it: firstly, that it meant, 'Moral condition especially as regards discipline and confidence', and, secondly, that I had been spelling it wrongly for a number of years. The longer I pondered the word 'confidence' the more I became convinced that morale, or state of mind, has a very great bearing upon many things other than war and industry: fishing for instance. Obviously, I reasoned, anything which will build up morale will help to catch more fish, and from that moment I was sold on 'morale'.

Looking back over my war service, I decided that morale was built up in two ways, namely, by ensuring that the material conditions of existence were conducive to a feeling of well-being, and by ensuring that things of the mind or spirit did not distract the man's thoughts from the job in hand.

Material comfort is catered for by supplying the fighting man with food, warmth, beer, 'vino', pay, a job which demands little mental effort, and one or two other things not appropriate to a fishing book. His spiritual well-being is catered for by leave, frequent letters from home, good leadership, Divine Service and so on. The important point is that physical well-being and mental alertness are usually present together. Let us see how these considerations can be applied to fishing.

Obviously, we are concerned with warmth, and we cannot do better than learn from the Royal Navy in this matter. The sailor on watch is often exposed to extremes of weather in positions where his movement is restricted. Under these conditions he wears long, machine-knitted underpants, 'bell-bottom' trousers of thick serge, long sea-boot stockings, and lastly sea boots at least one size too big. The upper part of his body will be covered by singlet, flannel (a kind of shirt) and a white 'submarine' sweater. This last item is semi-polo-necked and is long enough to go right down over the buttocks. As an outer garment and headcovering he wears one of the many types of oilskin: these are both waterproof and windproof.

The bank fisherman, sitting huddled on his basket in the chill of a February day, could wear with advantage an almost exactly similar rig. The fly-fisherman out in April could well use the long underpants and sweater, as the lower part of the back is particularly susceptible to cold. Being 'mobile', however, he cannot wear a heavy oilskin which would hinder his casting and movement generally, and he would do well to wear a sheepskin jerkin such as was issued as 'comforts' during the war. A large canvas pocket stitched on to the outside of the jerkin will hold an assortment of tackle, and preclude the necessity of lifting the skirt and letting in cold whenever cigarettes and matches are wanted. In wet weather the fly-fisherman will find the Army's very light and loose, short gas-cape a blessing. It has elastic cuffs and is sufficiently long not to drain off water into his waders. Being windproof, it is a surprisingly warm garment and it exerts no pull across the shoulders when casting.

All these items can be bought remarkably cheaply at 'Service Surplus' shops.

But for both the bottom and fly-fisherman there is one wet-weather garment which is as indispensably efficient as it is little worn (except at sea) and that is a towel worn as a scarf. Why woollen scarves are worn in wet weather I do not know: rain trickles through them in no time. A rough towel, on the other hand, is warm and will soak up water all day long.

I admit I am a little less practical about my headgear. Any kind of ear-covering helmet could not be considered since it would tend to prevent my hearing a rise. Again, I am a little superstitious: for fifteen years I have fished in the same very battered trilby and am sure I should fish at a moral disadvantage without it. My wife disagrees as wives do.

When the weather becomes more congenial, clothing must provide ventilation. Most aged fishing-jackets are sufficiently well ventilated without special attention, but if you order your suit 'full under the arm and easy in the scyes' it will lend itself to fishing much more readily when your wife at last forbids you ever to appear in it again.

Comfort is not only a matter of clothing: physical fitness must also be considered.

Some kind of training before opening day is a great help. The muscles of one's forearm are not in condition after a six months' closed season, and I like to get in at least two hours' hard casting practice on a couple of occasions just before the season begins. I find that excessive foot perspiration, which in April often results in cold feet when wading, can be prevented by dusting the feet with boracic powder when dressing. Cutting down perspiration is also good for the lining of your waders.

Nothing can be worse than a headache when fishing, and glare with its resultant eyestrain often leads to a headache. Polaroid glasses or goggles are a wonderful help, particularly if you will be fishing on the next day. But above all get a good night's rest before going fishing.

And what of the inner man! I find that sandwiches are unappetising, often, but I force myself to eat them. Any active sport demands energy, and energy results mainly from the breakdown of carbohydrates such as bread. Fruit is always welcome and chocolate, too, although the latter does tend to make one thirsty. In winter time a flask of soup or cocoa is my choice, but in summer time I prefer hot tea or black coffee. 'Fizzy' fruit drinks never seem to quench my thirst, and beer makes me feel drowsy on a hot afternoon so I leave them both alone when fishing. We all have to find out what suits us best.

That exhausts the subject of physical well-being, but we have not referred to the effect that our mental approach has on our fishing.

Occasionally we go fishing because we are worried and seek relaxation, and undoubtedly we come home better for our day by the water. But such a mental state is not a desirable preliminary to a good day's sport. To achieve success in any field of activity one's whole effort must be directed with complete singleness of purpose. Unfortunately, this modern world being what it is, complete freedom from worry seldom manifests itself – the angler usually has other things on his mind when he sets out for a day's sport. Nevertheless, it is surprising how much a wife can contribute to her husband's enjoyment by sending him out with a smile and a kiss after a good breakfast.

Much can be done to avoid annoyance accruing during actual fishing. Casts and points should be checked the night before, and rod-rings can be inspected and cleaned at the same time. Ferrules and lines also are best greased before setting out. During fishing, it helps to prevent future annoyance if you clear the eye of the fly of gut before putting it back in the box. There are hundreds of things which intelligent anticipation can do to prevent future annoyance. Small delays when fish are moving can try one's temper sorely, and at the very time when completely calm action is wanted something happens to make us incapable of it.

A pair of scissors is a necessity when fishing. How easy it is to produce them when they are attached by a 2ft lanyard to the buttonhole in the lapel and carried in the outer breast pocket! The round-nosed draper's scissors are the best type. Fastened as I suggest, there is no fumbling for them: you put your left thumb through the loop and pull, and furthermore you cannot lose your scissors.

Capt. L. A. Parker rightly suggests that good fishing is the result of taking pains. It applies not only to the fisherman's handling of his tackle but also to his handling of himself.

Let us then be anglers of 'high morale', able to fish hard and get the maximum satisfaction from our efforts; by so doing we gain confidence to tackle the problems of everyday life.

Plate XXI

By kind permission of C. E. White, Esq.

Blagdon Reservoir, a water renowned for its heavy fish. In the past, the high average weight was maintained at the expense of a relatively low production in pounds per acre.

Plate XXII

Thorpe Malsor Reservoir from the draw-off. This water is in need of restocking, but there is still a small number of large fish there, one of over 7lb being taken on the fly in 1950.

CHAPTER TWELVE

A Discourse on Lakes

FROM A FISHING POINT OF VIEW there are only two kinds of lake in which large trout may be expected to occur, namely: 'oligotrophic' lakes and 'eutrophic' lakes. A third type, 'dystrophic' lakes, in which the water is stained by peat and other organic matter, seldom contains any but small trout and is of little importance in our discussion.

The unfamiliar words are not of my choice, but they occur in many books about freshwater and were first used by Professor Theinemann. Their importance lies in their meanings: oligotrophic meaning 'little nourishing', eutrophic 'well nourishing', and dystrophic 'badly nourishing'.

It is important that the reader understand how and why these names are applied and I must therefore try to explain some of the behaviour of a body of water throughout the year.

Stratification

Water is at its heaviest when its temperature is 4°C. During the late autumn and winter, the surface-water of a lake cools to 4°C and sinks to the bottom and remains there, being added to by further cooling at the surface until the bulk of the water is at the same temperature. During spring the surface-waters are warmed by sunlight and are therefore less dense than the lower body of water. This upper layer is known as the 'epilimnion', the lower as the 'hypolimnion', and the narrow belt between the two, in which the temperature changes rapidly from that of the epilimnion to that of the hypolimnion is, not unnaturally, spoken of as the 'thermocline' (*vide* diagram 1).

The epilimnion is in constant circulation owing to wind action and is thus well oxygenated (see diagram in Chapter 9). The depth to which the upper layer extends is dependent upon the mixing effect of winds sweeping across the surface and possibly also on the depth to which the warming rays of the sun penetrate.

During calm weather when the epilimnion is not in circulation, there will be, during the heat of the day, a tendency for the fish to lie in the thermocline because of its higher oxygen content. Those who 'troll' in deep lakes are well aware of the fact that it is most important to spin their spoon or minnow at the right depth, but few realize

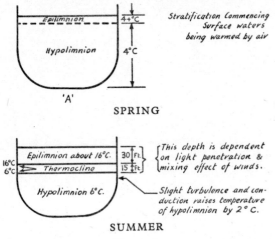

'A'

SPRING

SUMMER

Diagram 1

that they are in fact searching for the thermocline. A minimum ther-
mometer on a measured cord would help them to find the correct
depth without guesswork.

The epilimnion will remain intact until its temperature is the same
as the summer temperature of the hypolimnion, that is: 6°C. At this
point the whole of the water will have the same density and will be
readily mixed by the autumn winds as shown in Diagram 2.

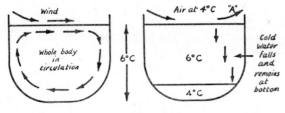

Diagram 2

Further cooling below 6°C results in the winter stratification shown
to be beginning in 'A' of the above diagram.

With the whole body of the water at 4°C, equal density throughout again permits of complete circulation as in Diagram 3. Cooling
below 4°C results in an insulating layer of water forming at the surface, since water near to freezing point is markedly lighter than
water at 4°C. When ice forms the water is protected from wind, and
further cooling of unfrozen water can occur only by conduction.
Thus a few feet below the ice, water is well above freezing point and
fish continue their normal lives.

In shallow lakes however, particularly in North America where winters are long and severe, a layer of snow over the ice may entirely prevent plants removing carbon-dioxide from the water, and in addition the oxygen may become exhausted; serious mortality in the fish population then occurs, and is known as 'Winter Kill'.

The slightest increase of surface temperature above 4°C in spring restores the position shown in 'A' of Diagram 1.

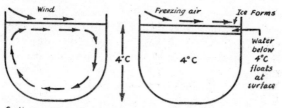

Cooling process shown at Diagram 2 "A" Completed.

Diagram 3 WINTER

Summarizing, we may say that during the summer the water becomes stratified into two distinct layers which do not mix: an upper warm layer or epilimnion and a lower cold one or hypolimnion. The region of the epilimnion where a marked temperature change occurs is called the thermocline.

Oxygen

Oxygen is acquired by water in two ways: first and most importantly by the diffusion of air into the water at its surface, and secondly by solution of the oxygen produced by green water-plants. The carbon of the carbon-dioxide dissolved in the water is used by the plant to form carbohydrates, and simultaneously a quantity of oxygen is released and can often be seen as small bubbles upon the leaves of water plants. This process only occurs in daylight and only plants whose cells contain the green pigment chlorophyll can use carbon-dioxide in this way. It must not be thought that plants 'breathe' carbon-dioxide, for they breathe-in oxygen and exhale carbon-dioxide, just as do all other living things except the anaerobes. But during day-time they use more carbon-dioxide to form carbohydrate than they exhale carbon-dioxide in the process of breathing. Carbon assimilation and plant breathing are two completely different functions going on side by side.

After the autumn water-mix has taken place and stratification is broken down the quantity of oxygen at all depths is approximately the same. Later, as decomposition of dead animal and vegetable matter takes place, the quantity of oxygen in the lower waters is reduced and by summer time the oxygen of the hypolimnion may be entirely used up. Thus there is not only a great difference in temperature between the epilimnion and hypolimnion, but also a chemical difference such that fish may be found in the former but not in the latter.

This phenomenon requires further explanation.

Plant Life and the Nutrient Cycle

Proteins are substances found in all living cells, and they are built up from over twenty different amino-acids. These acids are organic compounds, all of them containing carbon, hydrogen, oxygen and nitrogen, while some also contain phosphorus and sulphur.

The hydrogen and oxygen are supplied to the cell in the form of water, the carbon is extracted photosynthetically from carbon-dioxide, but the other substances must be obtained from soil-water in the case of land plants or from the water itself in the case of the small drifting plants, of which algae form the major part found in lakes and ponds.

Nitrogen is the most important of the protein-forming elements and it is never completely absent from the waters of the earth's surface. Even in complete absence of organic matter some nitrogen will be found in the form of nitrates, for whenever electric storms take place atmospheric nitrogen is combined with oxygen to give ultimately a nitrate. It has been calculated that in England about 8lb of atmospheric nitrogen are combined as nitrate in this way each year for each acre of land. In monsoon lands it reaches 80lb of nitrogen per acre or the equivalent of 4cwt of sulphate of ammonia. Nevertheless, in most waters the nitrate occurs principally as a result of feeder streams flowing through cultivated land from which soluble nitrates are constantly leached out in the drainage-water. Whenever animal or vegetable matter decomposes in the presence of oxygen, nitrate will be produced, thus all waters draining into a lake will carry some nitrate nitrogen.

In spring when surface waters warm up and stratification begins, the algae commence to multiply. If the quantity of nutrients is high the crop will be a big one; conversely, low nutrient supply will mean a small crop. The green algae use up the available nutrient until at last when one of the essential elements is entirely gone the 'crop' ceases to increase and starts to die off. It is not necessarily lack of nitrate which causes this decline. An investigation of Wisconsin lakes showed that a lack of carbon-dioxide which limited the production of carbohydrate was probably responsible, while at Windermere our scientists found that lack of silica probably limits the growth of diatoms. It is often difficult to assess the cause, for often a species of algae has started to decline when the dissolved nutrient seemed entirely adequate. It is now believed that some species produce substances which poison their competitors.

When these tiny plants die their soluble body nutrients pass back into the water. Some of them are completely decomposed by bacterial and fungal attack in the epilimnion, while the insoluble residues of others will slowly sink through the cold hypolimnion to the lake bottom. Here they are attacked by ammonifying bacteria and possibly later by nitrifying organisms, or they may be eaten by the bottom-dwelling animals. Whatever their fate the organic material forming their bodies is broken down to something simpler. It is because decomposition is carried out by living organisms that the oxygen of the hypolimnion is depleted while the carbon-dioxide content increases.

Meanwhile all is not static in the upper water: other algal organisms will have established themselves, reached a population peak and gone into a decline. There is a continuous rain of bodies from the upper water throughout the year. Sometimes the rate of deposition is so rapid that bodies are covered before they have decomposed, for in the low temperatures of the hypolimnion decomposition is always slow. If this should happen decomposition without oxygen, that is, anaerobic decomposition, must take place. This is extremely slow – in fact pollen grains over 1,000 years old have been recovered from the mud of Windermere, still identifiable. More dramatically, human bodies, centuries old, were brought up in excellent preservation from the mud of a small Norwegian lake. This preservation of proteins in the bottom mud means that the chemical nutrients they contain are lost to the water for all time.

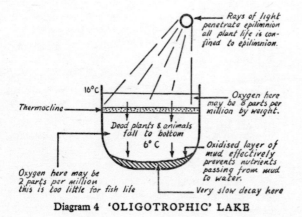

Diagram 4 'OLIGOTROPHIC' LAKE

When a lake is deep, the hypolimnion consists of a large volume of water whose oxygen will never be completely used up and the mud surface will always be in an oxidized state. This oxidized layer effectively insulates the water above from the products of anaerobic decomposition below. Such lakes will always be 'little nourishing' or 'oligotrophic', because they preserve their protein instead of breaking it down to simple plant foods for re-use.

But let us suppose that the lake is a shallow one perhaps only 50ft in depth. Such a water would form an epilimnion extending to a depth of about 35ft while the hypolimnion would be so small that its oxygen would soon be completely used up. The oxidized surface of the mud, a colloidal ferric complex, would then be broken down to the soluble ferrous state, and the nutrients locked up in the mud would pass through the mud surface into the water of the hypolimnion as illustrated in Diagram 5.

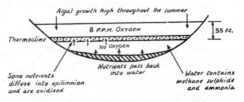

Diagram 5 'EUTROPHIC' LAKE

The absence of oxygen in the hypolimnion would mean that the products of decomposition would exist not as carbon-dioxide, nitrate and sulphate, but as methane (CH_4) ammonia (NH_3) and sulphide (H_2S). These noisome substances would not be oxidized until the autumnal mixing of the water, when these nutrients would be dispersed throughout the lake.

Although the epilimnion and hypolimnion do not mix during the summer, substances in solution in the lower layer will slowly diffuse into the upper layer. Thus during the summer, if the oxygen of the hypolimnion becomes exhausted the nutrient content of the epilimnion will be replaced to some extent, and algal production will continue at a higher rate than in an oligotrophic lake. Lakes whose hypolimnion oxygen becomes exhausted in this way are said to be 'eutrophic', because they 'nourish well' their upper productive waters.

In the case we have just considered a certain amount of nutrient does remain locked up throughout the summer and maximum productivity is never achieved. A water of about 30ft depth, or less, presents a very different and markedly more productive type of eutrophy. As with other lakes there is a spring 'flush'. During March and April,

Plate XXIII

A brace apiece by Col. S. W. Miller, M.C. and the author taken while fishing a few yards apart over a dense weed bed on August 11th, 1952. The fish weighed 1lb 15oz, 2lb 8oz, 2lb 6oz, and 2lb 7oz, and had been feeding on stickleback without showing at the surface.

high winds keep the whole water circulating and the bottom temperature will be similar to that at the surface.

The rate of decay at the bottom will be much higher than in a deep-stratified water, and as soon as calm weather settles in and the water becomes still, slight thermal stratification will occur and the bottom water will lose its oxygen. The nutrients of the mud will then pass into solution as in Diagram 5, and the next breeze will start the water circulating and disperse the nutrient throughout the water. This process may occur every few days and the algal production in the surface waters is correspondingly high.

Just to keep the story correct, I must mention that when a water contains much dissolved or suspended organic matter such as sewage or animal excreta the blue-green algae appear. Some of these organisms are able to use atmospheric nitrogen to make their body-protein and in this respect resemble some bacteria. When they die, their bodies decompose, and they therefore increase the nitrate of a water. Ordinary plants and algae can use only nitrate or in some cases ammoniacal nitrogen, the atmospheric nitrogen is no use at all to them. The blue-green algae are responsible for water bloom and also for odours and flavours in drinking water, and are therefore most unpopular with water-engineers.

The Productivity of Still Water

The algae are the basic food of all waters. Except where they exist as 'slime'-colonies upon weed-stems or rocks they are visible only as 'colour' in the water, but they are nevertheless the food of the small water animals such as daphnia, rotifers, hydra and so on, collectively known as 'Zooplankton', the plants being known as the 'Phytoplankton'.

These tiny animals are in turn the food of larger species and small fish, and these in turn are eaten by large fish. It should be obvious that the larger the algal crop the greater will be the production of fish. Thus the shallow lakes and reservoirs have an advantage over deep lakes, although some exceptions to this rule do exist.

It is most regrettable that we cannot remove from the water the whole of its crop of plankton.

Professor Juday found that the standing crop of plankton in Lake Mendota, an eutrophic water in Wisconsin, was 214lb of dry matter per acre. If we assume that the crop is replaced every ten days of the growing season, total production will be of the order of $1\frac{1}{2}$ tons of dry matter per acre per annum. Obviously such figures are approximations, but Worthington and Macan accept Juday's findings as being reasonable.

6

The analysis of this mixture of tiny plants and animals shows that 44·5 per cent is crude protein, 7·5 per cent is fat, and 48 per cent is carbohydrate. The protein-content is therefore equivalent to the protein in twice as heavy a quantity of high quality dried grass. Three tons of dried grass are worth about £84 at the moment of writing, and a crop of three tons could be obtained only from an acre of well-managed fertile land which had received manure.

The high fat-content of the plankton deserves some mention. John Clegg in his book *Freshwater Life of the British Isles* tells us that during the 1939–45 war German scientists obtained twice as much oil per unit of plant-nutrient from cultures of the Alga *Chlamydomonas* as was obtained from the same nutrient used for culture of oil-seeds.

In addition to the algal crop there is of course a crop of attached, higher plants. Professor Juday found that these grew to a depth of 23ft in Mendota and amounted to about 350lb of dry matter per acre of the whole water. This crop appeared only once a year and it was therefore deemed of less importance than the algal crop.

In very shallow lakes the standing crop of rooted plants per acre might well be much higher, and in fact it may, by taking up nutrient and holding it through the summer, restrict algal development.

Dr Gross writing in the July, 1941, issue of *Nature* tells of Allen's figures of 1915 which showed that the yield of protein from a Continental carp-pond was 20lb per acre heavier than the production of beef from grassland. Again, in 1939 the Munich fish-ponds yielded 400–500lb of carp per acre which compares very favourably with Wye College's 250lb live-weight increase for bullocks on each acre of land. The dressed carcase-weight would be only 60 per cent of this amount.

Whatever figures we choose we come to the conclusion that water can be amazingly productive and that its productivity ought to be exploited to the full.

Macan and Worthington have given us a 'magical' factor '7' in the food cycle of water. Each unit of vegetable food yields one-seventh as much animal matter. If this animal matter is itself used as food, it in turn yields one-seventh of its weight as fish. If a fish lived only on algae, 49lb of algae would produce 7lb of fish, but if the fish lived on small water-animals which in turn had lived on algae, 49lb of algae would yield only 1lb of fish. The result of this is, that a water with a given algal production will produce at least two and a half times as great a weight of carp-flesh each year as it will trout-flesh, since carp utilize plants for at least a part of their food while trout are almost completely carnivorous.

A typical unmanured eutrophic lake with a highly fertile bottom should produce in theory from 150 to 200lb of carp per acre per year or about 75lb of trout per acre. Oligotrophic water will usually have a much lower yield and might well be as low as 10lb per acre per annum. Stocking of water must obviously be related to productivity.

Utilizing Waters for Fish Production

If a water contained only phytoplankton and bottom plants the process of decomposition and regeneration of a 'crop' would be slow. The addition of small animals which eat the plants and excrete part of them as simpler organic substances would speed up the return of nutrients to the water. But the maximum rate of regeneration is achieved only when fish are added to speed the decomposition of the small animals.

The rapidity with which the excreted wastes of fish and the bodies of dead water-creatures are broken down into inorganic nitrate and phosphate is dependent upon the calcium content of the water. The bacteria which carry out the processes of ammonification and subsequent nitrification are most active at pH values above 6·5.[1] In addition Juday has shown that the carbon dioxide content of a water is dependent upon the amount of calcium present, and that where the calcium is low there may be a limit to algal growth by reason of carbon-dioxide deficiency. In Europe 65 parts per million of calcium carbonate and bicarbonate have been found to be necessary for the heavy cropping of water, and where waters are acid, up to 3 tons of calcium carbonate per acre may be added depending on the degree of acidity. Mild acidity itself does not harm the fish; it merely limits the natural productivity of the water and lowers the growth rate.[2] Quite

1. Neutral water is said to have a pH value of 7. Figures above 7 denote alkalinity, figures below 7 acidity. A fluid is said to be acid when the quantity of hydrogen ion (H+) is in excess of the hydroxyl ion (OH−).

pH means the concentration of hydrogen ion (in grammes per litre) expressed as the reciprocal of the logarithm. If a litre of water (1¾ pints approx) contained ·0000001gm of hydrogen ion we could express this small amount as a logarithm ie: 10^{-7} gr/litre. Usually in logarithms we omit the '10' (the base) and use only the index, in this case '−7'. The reciprocal of −7 is 7, thus we say a fluid containing ·0000001 gr/litre of hydrogen ion has a pH of 7 and is neutral. Since the figures are logarithmic reciprocals, a decrease of 1 unit means that the concentration of hydrogen ion has *increased* ten times. pH 5 is ten times as acid as pH 6 and contains 100 times as much hydrogen ion as a fluid at pH 7. pH 9 is 10 times as alkaline as pH 8 and contains 1/100th the quantity of hydrogen ion that a fluid at pH 7 contains.

2. Exceptions to the general rule, that acid waters do not rear good trout, are sometimes found. Lough Shure with water as acid as pH 4·8, little above the iso-electric point of many proteins, produces Rainbow Trout around the pound mark. The pH measurements were taken in May and August 1931. Presumably several measurements were taken at varying times of the day, though this point is not expressly referred to in Dr Winifred Frost's paper in *Salmon and Trout Magazine* of September 1940. It has been found in investigation of United States lakes that the pH value may vary by as much as 3 units in a 24 hour period, owing to removal of dissolved CO_2 from the water by photosynthesis.

obviously, calcium-deficient waters cannot support a large population of those species which construct their shells of calcium carbonate, and such species are an extremely important item in fish diet.

Following correction of the acidity it has been found profitable to manure with superphosphate or basic slag (this last itself corrects acidity). Krügel and Heinrich claimed that each pound of super-phosphate added to a water with an organic mud bottom gave an increased production of 2·13lb of fish. A normal dressing of super-phosphate is 1½cwt per acre per annum applied as ¾cwt in spring and the remainder in summer. When fertilizer is applied, a large algal population develops, and the resultant coloration of the water re-stricts the amount of light penetrating to the bottom and depresses the growth of attached bottom-plants. In deep water only the surface waters would receive sufficient light to produce algae, and the economical depth for fish-ponds has been found to be 6ft, ie: that depth of water in which the whole is actively productive. It is reason-able to suppose that a lake fishery could be made more productive by the application of fertilizer.

Fish Production in Reservoirs

We have seen how the dissolved plant-nutrients fed into a lake by feeder-streams are built up into vegetable protein and eventually into fish-flesh. The logical result of this is that the outlet-water from a lake contains less nutrient than the inlet-water, and the lake becomes a reservoir of plant-nutrients, its productivity increasing as the years pass.

If the lake is a water-supply reservoir this increase of productivity brings in its train a number of problems for the water-engineer, for the algal crop to be removed by filtration will increase with the in-creasing fertility of the water. Loch Katrine which supplies Glasgow with water is an excellent illustration of this, and it now produces a heavy algal growth quite unknown in the 1870's.

There are numerous ways by which plant-nutrient in a water can be reduced or controlled. The easiest is perhaps that used in stratified reservoirs, from which nutrients are easily removed by using the enriched water of the hypolimnion as compensation water. In shallow waters this method is seldom a practical proposition, and the methods employed include removal of a crop of fish, removal of organic mud, removal of marginal vegetation and, alas, the use of systemic poisons such as copper sulphate.

The removal of a crop of fish is the method advocated in pamphlet No11 of the Freshwater Biological Association of the British Em-pire (henceforward FBA). The writers suggest that removal of fish should absorb a very large part of the annual increase of nutrient.

Macan and Worthington in their book subscribe to this same view, and state that theoretically it is possible to check completely the accumulation of nutrient.

Where this means of control is to be used it is essential that the fish in the water shall have a high economic value. It is not enough for them to be nutritious if the angler finds them unpalatable. We possess an important sea-fishing industry, and coarse fish are here regarded as unfit for table.[1] The fact that the attitude may be a result of prejudice in no way alters the case, and the angler returns his catch to the water at the end of the day. The Continental approach to fish-farming cannot succeed in England until we confine our fish production to those species which find a ready sale: the salmonidae and eels. For removal of a crop of fish from a reservoir by angling, common sense dictates that the species stocked shall be trout, for such fish will always be retained by the captor and used as food. It is true that a crop of coarse fish could be removed by netting and subsequently used to stock the waters of a near-by Angling Association, but such a method has nothing to recommend it: nothing is contributed to the national larder; the sporting amenities of the neighbourhood are merely maintained but are not increased, and netting itself is an expensive and often unsuccessful venture.

The removal of mud and weed is of assistance not only to the water engineer, but also to the fisherman. Both operations are costly, particularly now that labour costs are much higher than before the war, and new methods of weed control are now being developed. The new hormone weed-killers will probably be used increasingly, but though they will restrict weed growth they will not remove nutrient, which being unused by attached plants may increase the algal crop.

All those who fish reservoirs should pay particular attention to the considerations of copper sulphate control. To be fore-warned is to be fore-armed, and I sincerely hope that any anglers who find themselves faced with the application of this method will bring its dangers to the notice of their elected representatives in local government.

When this damnable substance was first used it was applied at rates up to 10lb per million USA gallons (US gallon=8·3lb of water) and produced concentrations up to 1·2 parts per million. Hale carried out experiments and found that as little as ·14 part per million of copper sulphate was toxic to trout, while perch succumbed when the concentration was ·67ppm. Only Sun-fish and Black bass could survive a 1·2ppm concentration, and their survival is no triumph if they subsequently starve.

Fortunately, for the angler, it was found that following the use of

1. There is a limited market for carp to members of the Jewish community.

copper sulphate secondary growths of copper-resistant algae occurred. Some of these organisms were so tiny that they passed through the filter-beds, and the resultant spate of complaints from consumers that their tap-water was green caused engineers to modify their methods. Pamphlet No11 of the FBA reports on the work of Domogalla who used only ·05ppm of copper sulphate to control the algae of Lake Monona, Wisconsin.

Domogalla's method aimed, not at wiping out the algal growth, but at reducing the peak population to one which did not hinder filtration. That he succeeded in doing so is shown by population figures, but more important from the anglers' point of view is the fact that no secondary growths of copper resistant organisms took place and the protozoa and fish populations were undisturbed.

Most water engineers are loath to interfere with the biological balance of a water; nevertheless anglers may be faced with such disturbances of the fishery. Application of copper sulphate is not a job for a labourer: Domogalla's methods require very careful use of powder spraying equipment.

The Effect of Lake Type upon the Feeding Habits of Fish

Investigations of Swedish lakes by Alm showed that the weight of fish produced each year was approximately proportional to the weight of the available bottom feed. Fish production, he found, varied from 1 to 100lb per acre per annum while the standing crop of bottom-dwelling food animals varied from 1 to 215lb per acre.

It has been found that waters with peat or inorganic rock bottoms tend to be deficient in bottom fauna, and the bottoms described as being of 'organic mud' are those most productive of food animals. An organic mud is one consisting of finely-divided mineral particles, ie: silt or clay, together with plant and animal residues.

Under the best conditions this mud will exist as an ooze over the mineral bottom. The colloidal particles of this ooze play an important part in the adsorption of the cations of calcium, potassium etc, and in the adsorption of the phosphate anion. Where superphosphate is applied, the organic mud is of great economic importance by its retention of the phosphate ion which otherwise would be removed in the outflow from the pond. But for most of us this mud is important because it is a perfect environment for snails, mussels, worms and fly-larvae. In addition its rich supply of nutrients will give rise to an abundance of rooted plants which supply additional food for snail, and whose leaves and stems become covered with algae and protozoa on which other water-animals feed.

In ponds used for commercial fish-culture luxuriant bottom-vegetation is discouraged, but in fishing waters such plants are desirable. As a fish grows it tends to select larger food-forms. This fact is particularly true of trout and other carnivores. In a fish-pond, trout are seldom more than ¾lb in weight, and their diet of plank-tonic water-animals is adequate. But fish of, say, 2lb or over could not grow on such small organisms, for they would expend more energy in catching their food than was yielded from its assimilation and combustion. Large trout tend to be bottom-feeders and only an organic mud bottom can satisfy their demands for food species of sufficient size: caddis larvae, snails and other molluscs, corixa and so on. Very large trout are of course found in oligotrophic waters which are deficient in bottom-feed, but these fish have attained their size by feeding upon small fish which in turn have fed upon the small plank-tonic animals.

The food chain in such lakes would be, algae, protozoa, small fish and trout; and the addition of an extra link, again bringing in the factor '7', further reduces the fish crop.

Scale-readings of trout taken in two Midland reservoirs show that the fastest growth occurs in fish weighing from 1 to 2¼lb, that is to say, when the fish are big enough to take advantage of the supplies of stickleback. Over 3lb in weight the fish lose their beauty of form, probably because a stickleback diet is not a large enough food-form. In Lake Pend Oreille, USA, many Rainbow Trout over 30lb in weight have been taken. Many of these fish are but four summers old, and they are not ugly fish since they have access to a large enough food-species: a degenerate land-locked salmon about 6in long. If trout are to carry on growing while retaining their beauty, they must be able to select larger food-forms as they grow. It is possible that we could greatly improve the trout of the Midland reservoirs by using the true minnow instead of stickleback as a food species. Minnows can feed directly upon algae, whereas the stickleback is carnivorous. Thus the crop of food-minnows each year would be heavier than the stickle-back crop, and the use of minnows would provide a diet of greater variation in size, for large minnows weigh perhaps 8 times as much as large sticklebacks, while their fry are no larger. Their use entails none of the risks associated with large coarse species which compete with the trout for available bottom-food animals.

Summing up, we may say that eutrophic lakes will usually provide an abundance of bottom-feed because the bottom itself is rendered fertile by the deposition of large quantities of organic material from the surface water. Further, the relatively large area of the bottom receiving light from the sun will produce a heavy crop of attached vegetation among which heavy fish may find the large food-forms they require. In eutrophic lakes, trout can attain a weight of 4lb without resorting to cannibalism, and at that weight their diet will still include food-forms which can be imitated by a fly. The bottom-feeding habits of trout in eutrophic lakes will render them difficult to take on a dry-fly at the surface.

For the trout inhabiting oligotrophic lakes with restricted bottom-feeding facilities, surface flies are a more important item of food and in such waters the dry-fly may well give good results.

Angling in Reservoirs

Many keen trout fishermen remain, for years, unaware that their municipal water supply originates in reservoirs which contain trout. Angling friends living in my neighbourhood often ask me just where such trout are to be caught, and are dumbfounded when I tell them they came out of the local reservoirs. I myself, only twelve months ago, suddenly heard of a trout-water only fifteen miles from my home, which was hitherto quite unknown to me, and this in spite of the fact that this reservoir is a very large one.

I assume this ignorance has something to do with the fact that these waters and their environs are closed to the general public. The picnic-party and the trippers' charabanc seldom find their way to the waters, and thus they remain largely unknown. May I, therefore, suggest that you visit your local water office and find out just where your water comes from, and what fishing they have to offer. Sometimes you will find that the water is leased to a club or a syndicate, but usually you will find that it is fishable by permit, varying in price from 2s 6d to 12s 6d per day. Often the ratepayer receives especially favourable treatment. On one of the waters which I fish we 'locals' pay 2s 6d, while the 'furriner' pays 10s.

There are some reservoirs which are closed to anglers, and here the only possibility is to awaken the council to the possibility of increasing its revenue and the local sporting amenity.

Ignorance on the part of those in authority has caused many reservoirs to be closed to the angler. Macan and Worthington state that such closure is quite illogical, for standing waters inhibit the growth of harmful bacteria while the standard practice of chlorinating the water during its treatment entirely disposes of all risk.

The attitude of these water authorities is seen at its most absurd when we consider the unlikelihood of man-borne infection and the extreme likelihood of bird-borne infection. Gulls, it must be remembered, are frequent visitors to both sewage works and reservoirs, and they are not particular as to which they visit first. It is to be hoped that those authorities who dislike fishermen on their reservoirs introduce, and enforce, a rule to cover the bird menace.

Until two years ago the three reservoirs feeding a popular Devonshire resort were open only to season ticket-holders who presented a clean bill of health. Presumably a 'bill of health' from a day ticket-holder could not be relied upon! This confusion of ideas dates back to a 'typhoid' scare two or three years ago when the well-meaning but ill-advised Medical Officer of Health stopped all fishing. Let us hope that fishermen in this and other areas will seek to improve the education of their Water Boards.

With one or two notable exceptions, such as the Bristol Authority, there is a marked disinterest in the water from the fishing point of view. All too often there is no keen angler on the water-committee, and thus the authority never comes to realize that by providing good trout fishing it is providing yet another check on the purity of its water. If a water provides healthful conditions for trout it is unlikely to be an unhealthful water supply. In addition, the keen fisherman is quick to note and point out to the authority any foulness of the bottom. Perhaps some authorities fear this criticism but it is nevertheless plain that they should welcome it: for bad conditions for trout are almost certain to be bad conditions for the storage of water for human consumption.

More and more we shall have to rely upon these huge stretches of water to relieve some of the increased fishing pressure. Waters which are maintained by the general public ought not to provide merely week-end sport for a few wealthy members of a syndicate, or, as was happening five years ago in one case known to me, provide sport for one wealthy man. It is up to all of us to go into action against this sort of thing: these waters are our property.

The Midland Reservoirs

There is no doubt that the reservoirs of, and close by, the Midland Plain provide the cheapest good-class trout fishing in the whole of England. They are usually flooded farmland of high fertility. The soil is sweet, and thus the water is not acidified as it would be over marshland or bog. The dam is constructed across the headwaters of a river or tributary stream above all sources of pollution, and the incoming water is thus pure and well oxygenated. The Midland valleys are usually wide and shallow and thus the water forms a typical eutrophic lake with a fertile organic mud bottom. Many of these waters are no more than 35ft deep.

I am sometimes asked why it is that reservoirs constructed many years ago continue to produce large trout, while other lakes of a similar age will produce only poor stuff, and in many cases have become suitable only for coarse fish. The answer lies in a combination of factors.

By contrast with the ornamental lake a reservoir does not suffer from lack of cleansing. The weed is kept under control, and is seldom allowed to decompose in the water and take up valuable oxygen, while many lakes, uncleansed for years, develop thick beds of blanket-weed in their upper shallows.

In shallow lakes the value of weed lies in its power to remove excessive and harmful carbon-dioxide from the water during photosynthesis. The release of oxygen during the process is relatively unimportant, for this essential gas readily diffuses into the water at its surface.[1] Heavily weeded, shallow water may, at night-time, create actively poisonous conditions by its release of large quantities of carbon dioxide in normal respiratory processes, when no carbon dioxide is being turned into carbohydrate owing to absence of light. Certainly the decomposition of these blanketing weeds is a contributory factor to the deterioration of lakes. As the quality of the water drops over the years, so does the quantity of scavenging life in the water and with that the food supply of the fish. It follows then that when the rot sets in, it continues increasingly swiftly.

The reservoir has one tremendous advantage over the lake in that its level drops from 7ft to 15ft each year in high summer. In years of excessive drought, 75 per cent or more of the bed is exposed to the cleansing influence of sunlight and air.

It was many years ago that I read M. Louis Roule's book *Fishes: Their Ways of Life*, but I recall that he mentioned the emptying, drying, harrowing and manuring of Continental carp ponds. Most books on fish-culture stress the importance of an occasional drying of the pond bed and its resultant improved fertility. Our reservoirs receive at least a part of this treatment each year, and when the water rises in October and November it does not cover a growth of rushes, for these are mown and removed while the water is low.

In one respect, however, most of our reservoirs are seriously lacking, and this is in regard to spawning facilities. This problem is dealt with in the following chapter.

1. During hot weather on 28 August 1931, Birge and Juday found a layer of water at from 9 to 10 metres depth which was supersaturated with oxygen resulting from photosynthetic action of algae. Solar energy at these depths was found to be only 1¼ per cent of the surface energy. The oxygen content of this layer was markedly higher than that of water near the surface, and although no reference is made by the investigators to the presence of fish, there is little doubt that they would tend to be concentrated some 28ft down because of the high oxygen concentration.

CHAPTER THIRTEEN

Thoughts on Stocking

WE HAVE ALREADY SEEN that inland waters may be highly productive, and that the coarse species are unsatisfactory for reservoir stocking because they are a crop which the angler does not remove from the water. Nevertheless, whether or not they are introduced by man, they will inevitably appear after a few years, either entering the water from the feeder streams or as ova carried on the legs and feet of wading birds such as the heron.

In most eutrophic lakes, Bream, Rudd and Carp find themselves in an environment perfect in every respect, and being enormously prolific they will soon establish a heavy population. Brown Trout, on the other hand, produce only about 700 eggs per pound of body weight and furthermore, because their eggs must be covered by well oxygenated running water not normally found in most lakes, few of the eggs hatch out and natural regeneration is inadequate. For these reasons, trout in a lake populated with coarse species will be suppressed, unless good management and stocking maintain the supremacy of the trout.

In all problems of management we are faced with a lack of precise information on matters of every kind. Earlier, I mentioned Edward Hewitt's plankton theory, a theory worthy of investigation for Hewitt has been actively concerned with fisheries and hatchery management for most of his active life. He quotes a case of an experiment in England by Stratton Gerrish. A lake which provided an abundance of plankton feed, but few larger food forms, contained artificially reared trout which seldom grew to be more than ¾lb. A similar water stocked with naturally reared fish produced large trout which were plankton feeders throughout their lives. The substitution of fry stocking in the first lake resulted in the establishment of a plankton feeding population whose members grew to large size. If Stratton Gerrish's findings are generally true they are of enormous importance. The officers of the Freshwater Biological Association have no information on the subject and it would appear that no 'controlled' experiments have been carried out over here. United States sources are similarly devoid of information on the feeding habits of hatchery reared and wild fish. There was, however, a brief reference in the 1937 report of the US Bureau of Fisheries which may throw some light on the matter. Artificially reared Rainbow and Brook Trout were released in streams and later caught by angling. Examination of the stomach contents showed that the Rainbows had consumed large quantities of plankton in addition to insect food, while the Brook Trout contained only the larger food forms. On the face of it, the findings of Stratton Gerrish and the US workers conflict, but allowance must be made for the differences of habit of the species involved. On the available evidence I cannot accept it as proven that naturally reared fish are plankton feeders whereas hatchery fed fish are not, but I certainly feel that a full investigation would be worth while. In particular it might pay to investigate the feeding habits of Rainbow Trout and Brown Trout reared under identical conditions and placed in the same water. It has long been known that the active Rainbow can satisfy his appetite and thrive on smaller food forms than the Brown Trout, if in addition he can use plankton to supplement his diet his value as a species for stocking is greatly enhanced. It must be borne in mind, however, that habitat and the available food supply will have an enormous bearing on the diet of fish: in Lough Derg naturally reared trout are plankton feeders while in Lake Windermere they are not.

When I wrote my series of articles, I asked readers who had had experience of fry stocking in lakes and reservoirs to give me their views on the matter. Unfortunately no reply was received, probably because the method is seldom used. The liberation of fry into the main body of the water would be very wasteful, for such tiny trout need the environment of the feeder streams. These streams could be kept clean by a small 'header' reservoir higher up to provide an occasional flush in summer time, and small weirs about 18in high placed at intervals of a few yards would ensure a sufficient depth of water. Arrangements would have to be made to by-pass storm water direct to the main body of water by means of storm channels or the fry would be swept downstream after the first heavy downpour. The natural food supply could be augmented by the construction of weeded pools at the side of the brooks, and an occasional brief flush through these pools would result in small food animals being washed into the nursery stream.

The arrangement shown in Diagram 1 shows the basis of such a nursery. Protection from predators would be provided by wire netting over the top and a fish screen at the lower end. This type of stream would be ideal for spawning, particularly if the bottom were gravel, but I believe natural spawning would be more of a hindrance than an advantage because there would be no means of controlling the matings and ensuring that only desirable types of fish were perpetuated; neither would it be possible to control the number of fry in the stream.

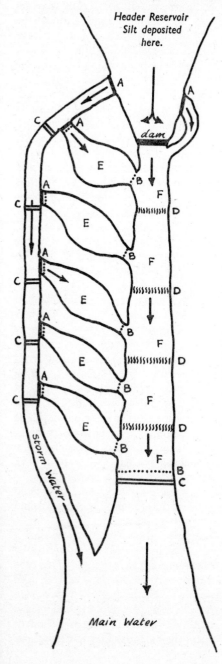

Diagram 1

Layout of Nursery Stream
For Rearing Naturally Fed Trout

A, sluice & screen. B, screen.
C, sluice. D, weir. E, shallow pond
stocked with weed, snail, freshwater shrimp etc. F, rearing pools.

Closing sluice C and opening A allows
screened water to flush through
ponds and carry food into rearing
pools.

93

It would be necessary to remove entirely the crop of fingerlings before planting a new season's hatch of fry in the nursery, and the use of the 'electric-fishing' apparatus now used in removal of vermin from small rivers would make a 100 per cent take possible. Marking the naturally reared fingerlings before stocking would enable the angler to identify them readily, and a contrasting marking system used on the normal hatchery-reared stock of the same age would enable comparisons of the two types to be made quickly.

The assessment of results is quite simple. The date of catching, weight and age are recorded for each fish and a table similar to the one below is prepared.

TABLE I

Hypothetical comparison of two stocks of marked Brown Trout

Total number of hatchery fish stocked: 400
Total number of naturally reared fish stocked: 400

Age of fish	Month taken	No of wild fish caught	Average weight	No of hatchery fish caught	Average weight
4	April	40	1lb 1oz	40	15oz
4	May	30	1lb 2oz	25	1lb
4	June	30	1lb 4oz	25	1lb 1½oz
4	July	15	1lb 6oz	20	1lb 3oz
4	August	15	1lb 8oz	15	1lb 5oz
4	Sept	30	1lb 9oz	20	1lb 6oz
Total		160		145	

Similar tables for older age groups would soon reveal the story. From such a table as that above it would be reasonable to conclude that the naturally reared fish were growing faster than hatchery reared fish, and in addition the numbers taken show that their recovery rate was higher. If this were also true in the other age groups it would mean either that the naturally reared fish were rising more readily to the fly or had a better survival rate. In either case they would be more useful fish. If, as is possible, the recovery rates were markedly different and the costs of the two types of stock similar it would warrant cutting out the one type of stocking entirely. Probably the best method of comparing the value of two methods of stock rearing is to divide the cost of rearing the fish by the total weight of mature fish caught, and thus arrive at the stocking cost for 1lb of each type of fish produced.

The Necessity for Marking all Fish

Tables such as the one above could not be compiled without data. The fishery officer or association managing the water must be able to identify each fish caught at a glance.

Scale reading is an exact science and the method makes it possible to calculate the length and weight of a fish at any time in its life if we know its length and weight when caught, for the weight of a fish varies directly as the cube of the ratio of its lengths at two stages of growth: if we multiply the length by 2 we multiply the weight by 2 cubed, or 8.

Let us presume that we have caught a fish 12in long and weighing 1lb. Scale reading and micro-measurement show the fish to have been 4 years old and the distance from the centre of the scale to the second annual ring to be two-thirds of the distance from the centre to a newly forming fourth ring or line of erosion. The ratio of the lengths of the fish at 2 years and 4 years will therefore be as 2 is to 3, and our 12in fish was therefore 8in long when 2 years old. Further, the cube of the ratio, 2: 3, ie: 8: 27, tells us that our fish at 2 years of age weighed $\frac{8}{27}$ of its weight when caught. $\frac{8}{27}$ of 16oz gives us its weight as having been $4\frac{3}{4}$oz. This method of calculation would be useful only when the conformation of the fish had not altered between the second and fourth year.

Useful though it is to know the past history of a fish, scale reading is of limited application in fishery management because it is a task for a trained worker. Its very exactness, resulting in limitation of the number of scales which can be read in a given time, is a serious drawback and for practical purposes we must have methods which can be used by the angler. Fin punching and fin-clipping are the best methods from this point of view.

A fish does not use its fins for locomotion but as stabilizers; even the tail is an unessential. The removal of a fin causes a young trout a little inconvenience at first, but within a day or two it learns to swim just as well as before. If a different fin is removed each year, the age of every fish caught is known immediately. Two systems of marking such as punching or clipping of the selected fin would enable two different stocks of fish of the same age to be separated for the purpose of making an analysis, such as that shown in Table I.

Once marking is undertaken effective management becomes possible; without it there can be no certainty, only guesswork. If the association members cannot trust themselves to remove a fin without damaging the young fish, it should be possible to obtain the fish suitably clipped by the hatchery workers, although this service would have to be paid for.

We most of us believe we know the answers to at least some of the following questions. But at the best our answers are inspired guesswork, at the worst they are hopelessly inaccurate.
1) Which survives the better, a fish stocked in spring or a fish stocked in autumn?
2) Which is it cheaper to stock, fry, yearlings or 2-year-olds?

3) How many fish are there in the water in each age group?

4) Do young fish rise more freely than old fish and do fast growers rise better than slow growers?

5) Is it weight or age which controls the trout's inclination to feed on the bottom?

6) Of two stocks of fish from different hatcheries, which has the better survival rate?

7) Of two stocks of fish, which grows the faster?

8) Of two stocks of Rainbow Trout has one a more marked tendency to migrate than the other, and does one tend to spawn earlier than the other?

9) Between what ages do the fish grow fastest?

10) What is the extent of natural regeneration of the stock?

After a few seasons' marking we could know all of these things.

At first sight it may not be easy to envisage how the answers to questions 3, 4 and 5 could be obtained. The method used is not 100 per cent accurate but it is considered sufficiently accurate by those engaged in deep-sea fishery research to warrant its use, and within the confines of a lake results should be more accurate than at sea.

A stretch of water is netted shortly before opening day, and the fish so caught are tagged and returned. In the case of a water stocked with marked fish, the number in each age group would be noted and the tag would be an additional marking; the fish would then be released in various parts of the water.

During the ensuing season some of the tagged fish will be caught, and the relationship of the number of tagged fish caught to the number tagged will be the same as the relationship of the total number caught to the total number in the water. The following table shows how the population is worked out.

TABLE II

Hypothetical Population Check

Age	Number tagged	Number of tagged fish caught	Total caught	Stock at beginning of season
4	50	15	300	$50/15 \times 300 = 1000$
5	45	13	200	$45/13 \times 200 = 690$
6	30	11	100	$30/11 \times 100 = 273$
7	15	3	40	$15/3 \times 40 = 200$
8	7	1	15	$7/1 \times 15 = 105$
9	2	–	–	– ?

Examination of such a table gives us a great deal of information. Firstly, by subtracting the total caught from the stock at beginning of the season we can find the number of fish in each age group remaining in the water. Secondly, we notice that the percentage of fish caught falls off sharply after the sixth year. In fact although we tagged two

Plate XXIV

The passage of time has mellowed Ravensthorpe Reservoir. Today, it is a water of unsurpassable beauty whose trout average over 2lb and at times rise very freely.

fish which were 9 years old, we have not caught any from this group, although judging from the number of 8-year-olds there should be a large population of 9-year-old fish. We could assume from our table that fish showed a tendency to become bottom feeders from the seventh year onwards and were no longer desirable in a water fished only by the fly. Such fish would be actively harmful for many of them would be capable of killing trout up to 1lb in weight. Our figures would in fact justify the removal of all fish over 6 years of age by any means available. Probably the easiest method would be to net them out when they ran up the brooks to spawn, but it would also be possible to spin for them during July and August. If this latter method were adopted it would be necessary to lay down a minimum width for spoon baits, or adopt a standard size and pattern: the use of 'Devons' would lead to the killing of too great a number of the smaller fly-rising fish.

We all like to feel that there is a chance of taking a ten-pounder on the fly – one was indeed taken at Shustoke Reservoir only a few years ago – but the chances of achieving this result are so small as to render idiotic the policy of allowing these large fish to remain in the water. In default of any figures or returns I would remove every fish of over 6lb from a fly water, and believe that there is a good case for allowing no fish of over 4lb to remain. I write this in all seriousness and with many memories of 'Dry Sack' to prompt me to write to the contrary. Even so drastic a step as this does not constitute the ideal policy as we shall shortly see.

How many fish shall we introduce to the water?

The aim of good management is to take the largest possible weight of trout from the water in such a manner that the population from year to year remains constant. As a rough guide, if the average weight of each fish caught remains at a satisfactory constant over a number of years the stocking policy is correct. If however the average weight increases the water is understocked. The converse also tends to be true, but it must be remembered that a revised stocking policy to remedy understocking will itself result in a decrease of average weight which may continue over a period of seven or eight years. Panic alterations of a policy should be avoided at all costs: overstocking of trout in lakes where natural regeneration is low is very easy to correct, either by netting or increasing fishing pressure.

Biological factors and matters of heredity govern the growth of fish by influencing the use the fish makes of its food, and it is not possible to get the same increase of body weight per pound of food fed at all stages of growth. In general, young fish tend to be better food converters than old fish, and a given water containing young trout in their most vigorous stage of growth would produce a greater weight of flesh each year than the same water containing older fish. Let us presume our water produces 100lb of fish food each season. Forty fish weighing 1lb each could eat 2½lb of food and perhaps gain 9oz each of body weight; thus the water would have produced 22½lb of fish during the year. On the other hand, ten large fish each weighing 4lb could each consume 10lb of food and perhaps gain only 1lb each, giving a total production of only 10lb of fish. Although the conversion ratios are not based on any experiment they are likely to prove true, for large fish require large food forms and the diet provided by the water, and which was so well suited to the smaller fish, would be unlikely to meet the needs of large fish; in fact the large fish might be unable to catch and eat the 10lb available to each of them.

Dr Meehean has stated that the culture of trout is comparable to the culture of any other livestock: I do not think many of us would quarrel with that statement, and yet we do not apply its implications.

Marking of fish and/or scale reading will show that in any given water there is a period in the life of the fish when growth proceeds very fast as measured by the total gain in body weight. In the two Midland reservoirs which I fish most frequently, scale readings have shown that the period of fastest growth occurs between the fourth and sixth years; thereafter the fish grow more slowly, probably because they cannot find a sufficiency of the large food forms required when they are over 3lb in weight. Under such conditions, perfect management would aim at removing all trout at the end of their sixth year, and all younger fish would be replaced to continue their fast growth. This method would result in a very heavy crop of fish each year, but it is obviously impracticable. As the corollary to cropping, the fish would be stocked as 'pounders' able to grow fast on the natural food supply of the water.

While agreeing that the ideal is unattainable because we cannot drain the water each year, we should not lose sight of the underlying aim: to ensure that the food supply is used by fish which can convert it into flesh economically. For many years Blagdon Reservoir produced only 3½ to 7lb of fish per acre, a ridiculously low figure for so fertile a water. The highest production for a similar water in recent years was 16lb per acre, still a very unsatisfactory return. At Blagdon the average weight of fish taken during the period of low productivity was around 3lb. In the other reservoir it was about 2¼lb. When the average weights are so high as these, it is inevitable that the angler will experience many blank days because the number of fish in the water is unnecessarily small. Many of the fish caught are, by reason of their great age, ugly and unpalatable. We most of us would prefer to catch more fish of a smaller size: fish which were beautiful to the eye and a pleasure to eat. These smaller fish also fight, weight for weight, far better than large fish.

In formulating a stocking policy we must estimate the productive capacity of the water and the rate of growth of the fish we are going to put in. It has been found that the annual weight increase of fish in a given body of water remains remarkably constant among individuals of the same age, and scale readings of the existing stock will therefore provide some facts to work on.

The table produced below is related to the conditions of a water which I fish frequently. For many years the stocking programme has been inadequate. Losses from natural causes are unknown, but herons and grebe are numerous and otters occasionally visit the water. Spawning losses are difficult to estimate but carcases are often found on the shores, whither they have been dragged by foxes or other scavengers. No matter what the manner of the removal of fish, all fish removed from the water must be counted as part of the crop. I have presumed a recovery rate of 50 per cent and a total productivity of 75lb per acre based on the known high nutrient of this eutrophic water on good agricultural land. I assumed that the heaviest natural losses would occur early and late in life, that the weight for age would remain much as it is now, and that equal percentages of each age group would be caught. Obviously some of the assumptions are invalid, particularly the last, and where common sense dictated, I adjusted the figures. I deplore such guesswork, but with so little factual evidence there is no alternative. The annual rate of stocking which appeared most likely to be correct as judged by the annual crop was 4,000 fish per year.

TABLE III

Probable Fish Population resulting from Autumn Stocking of 4,000 Brown Trout aged 1 summer, and fished at 50 per cent Recovery Rate

Col 1	Col 2	Col 3	Col 4	Col 5	Col 6	Col 7
		Av weight based	Gain during	Total	Number	Total weight
March	Population	on scale readings	previous year	gain	Taken	removed
yearlings	3500	1oz[1]				
2 summers	3000	5oz[1]	4oz	750lb		125lb
3 "	2700	10oz[1]	5oz	840lb		100lb
4 "	2500	1lb	6oz	940lb	725	725lb
5 "	1700	1lb 8oz	8oz	850lb	525	790lb
6 "	1150	2lb 8oz	1lb	1150lb	330	830lb
7 "	900	3lb 4oz	12oz	675lb	260	830lb
8 "	340	4lb	12oz	260lb	100	400lb
9 "	125	4lb 8oz[1]	8oz	65lb	40	180lb
10 "	70	5lb 8oz[1]	av. 1lb	70lb	25	140lb
Totals	15985			5600lb	2005	4120lb

(Col 2 annotations: "Under sized fish" for yearlings–3; "Takeable fish" for 4–10. Col 6: "Loss due to predators" for yearlings–3.)

1. Figures queried are either known to be variable or have not been sufficiently checked by scale readings. Old fish are sometimes found to be healthy and virile while others can barely put up a struggle.

The area of the water for which this table was prepared is just over 100 acres, and the total productivity would therefore be about 7,500lb per annum. The total gain in weight of the stock shown in the table is only 5,600lb per annum so that there is unlikely to be any overstocking while we remove 2,000 fish weighing about 3,900lb in addition to the 225lb removed by herons and grebes. Table IV, extracted from Table III, shows how the spawning loss is made up. No attempt has been made to reconcile the figure with the 1,500lb difference between columns 5 and 7: the difference is too small to be significant.

TABLE IV

Spawning Mortality of Age Groups 7 and over

Age	Number of dead fish	Weight of carcases
7 summers	300	975lb
8 ,,	115	460lb
9 ,,	15	70lb
10 + ,,	45	250lb
	Total	1755lb

The number of dead spawning fish is obtained by reconciling the March population and the number of that age group caught, with the March population of the next older age group thus:

March population of 7-year-olds = 900
Number of 7-year-old fish taken = 260
Number of spawning casualties = 300
Number of 8-year-old survivors = 340
Total 900

All in all I feel this stocking programme on the water concerned would give satisfactory results. If it is implemented, as I hope it will be, we shall have to wait at least four years and more probably eight to ten years before we can correctly assess its value. Natural losses may turn out to be smaller than we believe them to be; in which case we should find a denser population, and greater pressure on the food supply would result in the growth rate dropping very fast.

All stocking programmes should be kept well within the estimated productivity of the water because some of the nutrient supply is taken up by birds feeding on water weed, and by the removal of weeds after cutting; neither must we forget the loss of nutrient in the water supplied to the filter beds. Any means by which the plant nutrient is reduced occasions a proportionate lowering of the annual fish crop. There is a real necessity for ensuring an adequate scale of nutrition for the fish, and preventing the outbreaks of disease consonant with near starvation.

Scientific Publication No6 of the FBA gave Schaperclaus's tables for the productivity of waters stocked with carp. These figures are too high for use in this country where the summer is shorter and cooler than in Germany. I have scaled the carp figures down to obtain a figure for trout production, based on the probability that trout production would be rather less than two-fifths of carp production. The figures also take account of our shorter summer.

TABLE V

Probable Yield of Trout in Shallow Lakes

Nature of water supply	Nature of lake bottom	Annual yield of trout in lb/acre	
hard	organic mud	60 to 75	*see following*
hard	inorganic	40 to 60	*paragraph*
soft	organic mud	20 to 40	
soft	peaty	10 to 20	

While yields of 75lb and more are theoretically possible, the heaviest crop of trout actually taken from any unfertilized lake in Britain appears to be the 60lb per acre per annum from Bury Lake, Chesham. In this water the maximum depth is only 4ft, and conditions are as near perfect as is possible. Natural spawning is discouraged and the whole stocking programme is rigidly controlled. The lake is managed as a Rainbow water, although a few Brown Trout are also stocked each year.

In large reservoirs such good control of the population is impossible, but while in the most fertile water 60lb per acre may be out of reach 40lb is not, and we ought to be very dissatisfied with yields of under 20lb per acre. The term 'hard water' in the table above means water with over 65ppm of calcium carbonate or equivalent bicarbonate. Soft water is that having less than 65ppm.

In private lakes the use of superphosphate fertilizer would enormously increase the productivity of the water. Heinrich and Krügel found that each pound of 'supers' gave an increased yield of $2 \cdot 3$lb of carp, so it would be fair to assume that in a lake having an organic mud bottom and a supply of calcareous water, each pound of superphosphate should increase yield by 1lb of trout.

How and When Shall We Stock?

'The worst enemy of a little trout is a big trout.'

If there is one time when big trout are less interested in food than any other, it is over the spawning period. During the spring and early summer they are most active in their feeding, and would probably then indulge in cannibalism whenever opportunity occurred. Herons and grebe are also to be seen fishing hard in the spring, particularly when they have growing broods to feed.

Both fish and bird predators find spring-stocked trout easy meat. When placed in the water the youngsters often remain in a shoal, undispersed, for as long as three weeks. This may in part be due to their habit of life in the hatchery where there was no need to search for food, but I do not believe this to be the sole influencing factor: I have long believed that all trout show shoaling tendencies in still water. Early in the 1952 season we located a shoal of 6in fish cruising fast near the corner of the dam. Since we had stocked with 8in fish in 1951 we were inclined to believe that these were the young of a coarse species which had found its way into the water. Fortunately, I rose and hooked one on a tiny dry fly, and although it kicked itself free, its behaviour readily identified it as a small trout. These fish must have been bred naturally and hatched out in the spring of 1951. But although these wild fish were moving as a shoal, it was a very small shoal moving over a wide area and therefore unlikely to be subjected to continuous attack.

Just how serious can be the losses by predation is well illustrated by what occurred at a Midland reservoir several years ago. In early spring, 1,500 yearlings were placed in the water near the corner of the dam. At the time of delivery, the water-keeper, who was not expecting the fish, was engaged upon his duties around the catchment area and was therefore unable to prevent the whole lot being placed in the one spot. Within two hours, he later told me, seven grebe had arrived upon the scene, and these continued harassing the guileless young trout until the shoal broke up days later. A 50 per cent loss of the new fish in the first seven days after stocking was extremely likely in this particular instance.

A little research on the relative values of autumn and spring stocking has been done in the United States. Autumn stocking in rivers has been shown to give very poor results, particularly in mountain streams; but in lakes excellent results have been achieved, recovery rates being at least as good as those with spring stocking. Because of the dangers of loss due to predation it is imperative that yearlings enter the water in the autumn. Spring stocking with yearlings is a waste of money, and should give way to stocking fish at least 8in in length; in the long run, however, autumn stocking of yearlings will prove the cheaper proposition.

The fish should be introduced, twenty-five or thirty at a time, at points all round the lake. Near-by cover in the form of weed beds, tree stumps and so on is a great advantage to the young fish. Never should they be dumped in one spot.

A short while ago I came across a case where it was decided to omit the year's stocking, because fewer fish than usual had been caught. In some seasons, takes will fall below normal and the two possible causes require quite different treatment. To cease stocking means that the fishing in three years' time and onwards will be adversely affected, and yet unless a marking policy has been in force for some time this may be the only safe thing to do. A marking policy enables one to assess the cause of the small catch. The most usual trouble is a very cold or very hot summer, in which case the percentage of the total catch for each age group will be found to agree closely with the percentages of previous years. This would mean that the fish population had not suffered any disaster and was in excess of its usual end-of-season strength. The remedy is, to net a stretch of water and kill sufficient fish of varying weights to bring up the annual crop to its normal figure and then continue the usual stocking programme. If on the other hand it were found that the number of fish caught was well below normal because the lowest age group had not contributed its usual quota to the total, then this may be taken as clear evidence that the stocking of the group was followed by severe mortality, and in this case the normal stocking programme should be continued since the water is already understocked. Pollution of reservoirs is unlikely to occur, but if such mishap does take place then it will do so during the summer months when the dead fish will be found and will tell their own story. If subsequently the season's catch is below average, it may be assumed that many fish have been killed and the stocking policy should be continued. I would not, however, advise an increased number of stocked fish for they would hinder the re-establishment of a normal population.

Vermin Species

Darwin in 1856 stated that the manner of increase of any species was a geometric progression, but that the total population was limited by the available supply of food and the action of parasites and predators; thus we may say that a given environment will be found to support a vermin population which remains remarkably constant from year to year whenever the control methods are not aimed at complete elimination. The classic examples of failure of attempts at control are to be found in the case of the rabbit and the rat.

Shooting, trapping, ferreting and snaring have merely resulted in a temporary reduction of the rabbit population. Whatever good has been achieved has been entirely offset by the fact that the survivors with less competition have multiplied at a higher than normal rate and brought the population back to its previous 'high' in a very few months. Campaigns against the rat have followed much the same course and with similar results.

In America and Canada the bounty paid on certain predators such as the coyote has had little effect on the populations. Year after year the bounty money paid out has been a fairly constant sum, due to the fact that the number of animals killed is approximately the same each year. Today the conservation officers and pest control officers understand why their past efforts have met with failure and they are directing their attacks on undesirable species in new ways.

The method used by the forestry officer against rabbits is the complete extermination of all the rabbits within an area enclosed by a rabbit-proof fence. Recently, a forestry officer told me that it had cost £55 to kill the last rabbit in a clear felled area which had been due for replanting. But since it was still free from rabbits and none of the thousands of young trees had been damaged he deemed the money well spent.

The other method of control is that of changing the environment to render it unsuitable for the vermin species under attack. The rat is now being controlled by just such means. Farmers and warehousemen are rat-proofing their food stores; householders clear up food scraps; holes and cracks in walls are sealed up, and life is made difficult for the animal. Undernourished and lacking protection, the rat has to extend his feeding range and is thereby subjected to attacks by his natural enemies. His lowered plane of nutrition results in a lowered rate of reproduction: the rat menace is now under control. The same methods are also being brought to bear against the rabbit. The increased use of the combine harvester has led to the removal of the hedges and banks in which the rabbit made his burrows, and on many farms rabbits are becoming extinct.

Perhaps, reader, you wonder what all this has to do with fishing.

Most of our fisheries have a vermin problem. In the Test it is grayling; at Windermere it is perch; in the Yorkshire streams it is chub; at Ravensthorpe it is rudd, and so we could carry on indefinitely. In most waters the coarse fishes thrive because in addition to their prolificacy they are better able to withstand the low oxygen content of the water in the summer months, and are less susceptible to the toxic substances in the effluents which find their way into the water. Very shallow lakes, whether the water be healthful or not, usually provide a better habitat for the relatively valueless coarse species than they do for trout. Let us face the truth, the trout goes under because the environment has changed against him. If a water is being polluted, control of the vermin is pointless for trout will not thrive in polluted waters even if they are the sole occupants. In a case like this the first step is to clean up the water and think about the vermin afterwards.

Until very recently, attacks on the vermin species of fish have followed the same course as past attacks on the rabbit and rat. The waters have been netted; a lot of useless fish have been removed, and a few have been left behind to restore the population rapidly. Man has done nothing except prevent the vermin species competing within its own ranks.

A trout water close to my home has contained rudd for over fifty years. Before the war, thousands of fish were removed each year by netting, and yet the population from year to year was roughly constant, fluctuating only according to the natural population cycle of the species. Exactly the same sort of thing is happening at Shustoke: netting will never be the answer, and indeed it cannot be because it fails to take into account the fact that the vermin population is controlled by the environment and not by removal of a percentage of the members.

Any method of control which falls short of an extermination policy is fore-doomed. Let me tell you what happened when the lake mentioned above was partly drained during a drought. When there remained but a small area of water this was thoroughly netted and the very few rudd present were removed. Subsequently the lake was refilled. The following year we caught adult rudd! I can only presume that they had undergone a period of dormancy in the mud. But whatever the reason for our failure, it would appear to be necessary to drain, dry out and plough the lake bottom if the opportunity to do so should present itself again.

A reservoir cannot be emptied merely because the coarse fish are a nuisance, and most water authorities do their best for the angler by bringing out the nets and effecting a temporary reduction in the ranks of the coarse fish. Quite recently I attempted to obtain the services of a gang of netsmen to clear some of the fish from a reservoir. I found that the task could not be undertaken during the coarse fishing closed season. Requests for aid elsewhere met with the same astonishing reply. In an 'off the record' conversation with the extremely able secretary of a very famous fishing organization I found that the netting authorities frowned upon the disturbance of the coarse fish during their spawning season. I can appreciate their point: they want to take the fish out and use them to stock other waters without serious mortality to the gravid fish. But from the point of view of the trout fisherman the idea is not a good one because he has to put up with the shoals of fish in the shallows during the early season and then when their spawning is over the shoals break up and heavy hauls of fish are difficult to take. Many reservoirs are over 30ft deep and netting can only be fully successful when the shoals are spawning in the shallows. In any case what is the point of removing the parent fish after they have successfully spawned and sown the seeds of a new crop?

My dissatisfaction led me to consider other methods. 'Electric

105

Fishing', as yet in its infancy, offered no solution. The latest German machines can operate in water up to 9ft deep but this is of little use in a reservoir, likewise it is hard to see how electric fishing could be used for 100 per cent results in a lake. I then recalled an article on selective poisons which appeared in *Fishing Gazette*.

The substance referred to was Rotenone, the active principle of the Derris used by every gardener for controlling greenfly. A letter to the Ministry of Agriculture and Fisheries elicited the information that it was a most effective poison, but that I would be liable to a fine of up to £50, or up to three months' hard labour, if I used it.

The relevant section 9(b) of the Salmon and Freshwater Fisheries Act of 1923 no doubt serves a useful purpose, and would appear to be occasioned by the danger of poachers using poisons for highly improper purposes. But there are undoubtedly occasions when fish poisons could be used for the improvement of a fishery. Most drugs can be used for improper purposes, and the officers of the law rightly act with firmness against those who traffic in drugs, but there are many ways in which these selfsame drugs are used to benefit mankind. Rotenone remains barred to those who would use it to good purpose. Whether or not the law will be amended in view of the extensive use of Rotenone in the United States I cannot say, but it is possible that the River Boards may have power to make recommendations, and it is to be hoped that they will interest themselves in this aid to good fishery management.

The American Fishery Leaflet No350 also reveals a certain hesitancy on the part of American authority in the acceptance of a new approach to an old problem. The opening sentence runs as follows: 'The laws of all states prohibit the use of Derris, or other poisons to fish, in public waters'. Having thus covered himself, the writer then goes on to tell the reader how he may achieve the best results with the substance.

Very low concentrations of Rotenone are toxic. The application of only 1·4lb of Derris (5 per cent Rotenone) per acre foot of water, as advised in the leaflet, results in a lethal Rotenone concentration of 0·03ppm.[1] The poison causes constriction of the capillaries of the gill filaments and consequent asphyxiation of the fish. Before the substance can be used the quantity of water in the lake must of course be calculated. Because of the rapidity with which a vermin species will repopulate a lake it is probably wise in the long run to poison out the whole water, trout included, and start all over again. In large lakes,

---

1. The American pamphlet probably contains a misprint. In one paragraph it advises ·5ppm of Rotenone. It is probable that it should read ·5ppm of Derris, since this gives a ·025ppm concentration of Rotenone which is approximately the concentration achieved by distributing 1·4lb of Derris per acre of foot of water.

however, a 100 per cent kill is unlikely and selective poisoning would then appear to be the best compromise. The method relies upon the fact that when the temperature of the surface waters rises above 65°F the trout will seek deeper water which, being cooler, will be better oxygenated. The coarse species on the other hand will often remain in very shallow water, and spraying of the shallows in the noon heat will result in the poisoning of the vermin while the trout remain unharmed. The trout will not normally re-enter the marginal shallows until evening time and by then the concentration of Rotenone will have been reduced by dilution with unsprayed water. This method should be very effective in dealing with shoals of fry.

It has been found that fish affected by Rotenone rapidly recover when placed in a tank of uncontaminated water. It would thus be possible to render first aid to the occasional trout. The carcases of the coarse fish may safely be fed to stock, and in any case should be removed from the water. Being non-poisonous to farm stock, pets and human beings, Rotenone is safe for use on a reservoir, and has a great advantage over copper sulphate in that the small water animals and plants appear to remain unaffected by it. Rotenone offers new hope to those who fish vermin-infested trout lakes: but its use in rivers could be disastrous.

Before I pass on to other matters, I would emphasize that I would never advocate the poisoning out of a coarse-fishing water unless the water itself would support a trout population and the measure were supported by the anglers who fished the water. Where a trout population is subjected to competition from undesirable coarse species the end justifies the means. Rotenone cannot give good results unless its application is very carefully supervised and the habits of the species to be controlled are thoroughly understood. I advise any interested readers to obtain and read the American leaflet themselves, and to seek advice from their River Board.

Basic Facts about Animal Breeding and Our Fish

If today your butcher supplied as the Sunday joint a piece of mutton from the type of sheep grown in Britain two hundred and fifty years ago, you would not be grateful to him despite the present meat shortage. A joint from Bakewell's 'Leicester' sheep, or from Ellam's improved 'Down' sheep of the 1780's would be a very different proposition, for the lean meat would contain much more intermuscular and intramuscular fat and the resultant roast would be deliciously tender.

Our poultry, cattle, rabbits, pigs, horses and sheep have all been improved by selective breeding, and until recently the method used consisted of the breeder mating two animals of the type he deemed most nearly perfect. From the progeny he again selected the animals which best suited his purpose and used them either for brother and sister mating, or crossing back to sire or dam, or other inbreeding method, until eventually he had a strain of sheep or cattle which would produce young which were all of the type he desired. If the original parents had been of differing breeds, the new true-breeding progeny would be a new breed. If however they were of the same breed and the farmer had merely set out to improve his stock, we should say he had produced a new strain or race.

Bakewell in the 18th century was considerably ahead of many of today's farmers who will buy and use a young stud animal merely because it has a pleasing body conformation. Bakewell found that it frequently happened that an animal of inferior appearance sired better progeny than another animal of apparently better quality, and before he died he made a practice of hiring out his rams to serve the ewes of a neighbour's flock. If the ram produced good lambs of the type Bakewell wanted, he brought the ram into one of his own flocks, and conversely a ram which sired poor quality lambs would remain for hire. Bakewell assessed the value of a breeding animal by the quality of the stock it sired, not by its own appearance. His method, now known as progeny testing, is coming back into use in this country following the success which the Danes have achieved with it.

But although breeders are now becoming interested in progeny testing, the stud animal is still the result of in-breeding because it is desirable that he produce stock of consistently high quality. It must be faced that in any system of the mating of close relatives there must be as many cases of the bad qualities of the parents being combined as there will be of only the good qualities combining, and there must also be a number of offspring in which good and bad qualities will be mixed. I do not wish to embark upon a discourse on 'genetics', the science of inheritance, for that is outside the scope of this book and is a job for the man who has made a life study of the subject, but it is important that you, reader, should appreciate how inheritance works, for the basic facts of breeding a milking cow apply equally well to breeding a trout.

The unit of inheritance is an infinitesimally small amount of chemical substance called a gene. Genes exist in chains called chromosomes and a number of chromosomes are found in the nucleus of every cell of every living thing. Except in certain cases the chromosomes exist in pairs and the genes being always in the same order lie side by side. That is to say, a gene controlling hair colour will be paired with a gene which also controls hair colour, though not necessarily a gene giving the same hair colour. Of each pair of chromosomes one is inherited from the male parent and the other from the female, and the appearance and behaviour of an individual depend on the way the inherited genes interact, but we must also remember that environment too plays an important part.

Let us suppose that A represents a gene for fast growth and A_1 a gene for slow growth (or, if you prefer it, absence of a gene for fast growth). A fish descended from true-breeding fast growing parents would be fast growing and would have the constitution AA. Another fish descended from true-breeding slow growers would have the constitution A_1A_1 and would itself be slow growing.

In the production of ova and milt, there is a halving of the chromosomes in the cells which results in each egg or sperm containing only one set of genes. Such a cell is called a reproductive cell, and in the case of a female fish of constitution AA all eggs would carry the factor A for fast growth, while the male fish having the constitution A_1A_1 would produce sperms each carrying the factor A_1 for slow growth.

The diagram below shows the mating of these two fish.

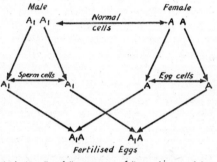

All body cells of the progeny of the mating must have the constitution A_1A

Diagram 2

The progeny of this mating will all carry the factors of both slow and fast growth, and if neither factor is more powerful than the other, the progeny will have a growth rate intermediate between that of the two parent fish.

But now let us suppose that A is 'dominant' to A_1, that is to say the power of the fast growth factor overcomes the influence of the factor for slow growth. Our fish with constitution A_1A would then be fast growing, but as shown below could not breed true. In Diagram 2, only one type of gene combination was possible because each parent produced only one kind of germ cell. Parents with A_1A constitution, however, will produce equal numbers of A germ cells and A_1 germ cells, and because the union of sperm and egg is quite haphazard the ordinary laws of chance result in three types of progeny being produced in a predictable ratio.

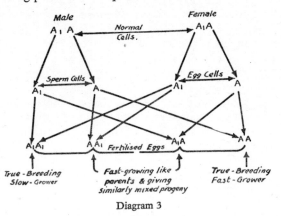

Diagram 3

Thus from our fast-growing parents we have produced 25 per cent of slow-growing fish and 75 per cent of fast-growers and of these fast-growers only 25 per cent will breed their like. The only way in which the breeder could pick out the true-breeding fast-growing fish would be to mate several male fast-growers to a slow-growing female whose eggs have been separated into as many batches as there are males. Any batch of progeny which contains slow-growing fish must have come from eggs fertilized by a male which carried the factor for slow growth. Such a test would only be valid if the factor for fast growth were completely dominant.

If before using a pair of fish for breeding it were necessary to test the quality of their offspring, it would mean waiting an extra twelve months before either of them was used to breed fish for stocking, but until we do accept this delay we are unlikely to find the best combinations of parents.

A hen fish produces about 1,500 eggs when she weighs 2lb and it would be possible to split the eggs into ten batches, fertilize them with milt from ten different males and observe the rate of growth and other characteristics of the progeny. All progeny would need to be kept separate, but under identical environmental and feeding conditions. With ten hen fish and ten males, 100 combinations are possible, and in the following season one could mate the fish giving the best quality progeny.

If, reader, you are an animal breeder you will know that I have over-simplified the matter of inheritance. The characteristic of fast growth might easily be controlled by a dozen or more genes, and in mating the number of combinations possible would make it extremely difficult to recognize differences between one fish and another. Nevertheless, the principles underlying breeding problems remain the same and systematic work will have to be undertaken before progress is made. I have mentioned fast growth as being a desirable quality in a fish, but it is not the only or even the most desirable quality as will become apparent when I refer to the breeding work carried out with fish in the United States.

Heredity, unfortunately, is only a part of the story, for environment has an enormous influence on all living creatures. If a fish with a constitution for fast growth is given or can obtain only a small amount of food each day, it may well be considerably smaller at the end of the growing season than a fish with a constitution for slow growth which has been given as much food as it will take. In other words, to get the best results from our breeding work we must feed our fish up to their genetic capacity. But although the fast-growing fish on a starvation diet may have appeared insignificant by the side of his less well bred physical better, in breeding work he would be a much more valuable fish, his genetic constitution being uninfluenced by bad feeding.

The food which a fish eats can be divided into two parts, the maintenance ration which enables it to live in a state of rest, merely holding its place in the stream and keeping its organs functioning, and a production diet which is expended as energy for movement and metabolized as flesh and fat. The longer any animal takes to reach a certain size, the greater becomes the proportion of its total food which is used for maintenance. Conversely the greater the percentage of food used in making flesh, the more cheaply can the animal be raised to the pre-determined weight or size.

The measure of the economic value of a fish which is raised in a hatchery is the cost to raise 1lb of flesh as compared with the price for which that flesh can be sold. Because fast-growing fish will always use a greater percentage of their food for flesh forming, they must always be cheaper to produce than slow-growing fish, just as a fast-growing beast is a more economical producer of beef than a 'poor-doer'.

There are possible objections to this reasoning and the first is that a fish is a cold-blooded animal and does not waste flesh in the form of surface heat in winter time as does a store beast on an inadequate winter diet. The second is, that one may deliberately hold an animal on a low plane of nutrition and then fatten it when the high quality foodstuffs required are cheaper. But neither objection is valid, for no matter what the system of management the fast-grower must always produce its flesh with a greater economy of food than the slow-grower.

I have posed this matter of food and growth for a very simple reason: so far as I am able to discover no work to improve our trout has ever been carried out. The advertisers in our angling magazines draw attention to the fact that their stock is bred from wild fish as though this in itself were some wonderful achievement. What the advertisements mean is that the stock is of mixed origin and variable in type, and possibly that the hatchery does not go to the expense of feeding the parent fish to maturity. I can think of but one type of water which might require to be stocked with the progeny of wild bred fish and that is the moorland stream, and here again there is no proof of necessity. If hardiness were important it is more than likely that the hatchery rearing would do much to destroy the very qualities which made it necessary to use wild parent fish, just as the offering of foodstuffs to Dartmoor ponies and hill sheep would tend to encourage them to rely upon man rather than upon their own ability to find their food under all conditions. It is strange too that the fish breeders should place emphasis on heredity in this one respect and ignore it in all others.

Moorland streams usually contain enough fish without any stocking at all, and there is no doubt that 50 per cent of the wild bred stocks are placed in waters which provide them with better feeding conditions than they knew in the hatchery, while another 20 per cent will be no worse off. To put fish bred from wild parents into highly productive waters is as wasteful as using a first class lowland pasture to rear and fatten slow maturing hill sheep.

Experiments with Trout in the United States

It was in 1919 that Embody and Heyford commenced their series of experiments on the inheritance of the capacity for fast growth. By 1926, their work at Hackettstown Hatchery, New Jersey, had proved that it was possible to raise strains of fish which grew much faster than wild bred fish. By mass selection of their breeding stock over three generations they raised the average length of Brook Trout at 1 July from 2in to 4in. The improvement meant that the new strain was able to increase its weight to eight times as much in the same growing period. (You may check this by applying the rule regarding the cubing of the ratio of the lengths.)

In 1928 another series of experiments was commenced at Pittsford, Vermont, under Davis and Lord, who replaced mass selection of breeding stock by individual matings, and by this means were able to observe what characteristics were inheritable and the extent to which given fish transmitted their own characteristics to their progeny. In other words Davis and Lord were progeny-testing their fish.

In 1930, the selection of the forty-five pairs of breeding stock of the second generation was carried out on a basis of rapid growth, vigour, fecundity, body symmetry and coloration. In practice it is impossible to improve more than one characteristic at a time and the breeder would therefore select his fastest growing fish which were satisfactory in all the other respects, he certainly would not use any fish which lacked vigour or prolificacy or was abnormally shaped, no matter how fast it grew. Insistence on these other desirable characteristics ensured that the improved strain of fish was viable and capable of breeding to perpetuate its type. The progeny of these matings were tagged and it was thus possible to trace the ancestry of every fish raised.

One of the points noticed at the mating of the second generation fish was that they each tended to come into spawning condition at the same time as their parents had done, and that the duration of their spawning period was similar to that of their parents. By 1933 all doubt had been dispelled: consistently, fish had become 'ripe' at the same time of year as their parents, and furthermore, once having spawned at a certain date they continued in later years to spawn at approximately the same date. In two cases the coming into spawning condition of the progeny had coincided to a day with that of the parent fish.

In point of fact there were two types of improvement going on at Pittsford, for fish which were not good enough for individual matings were used for the production of fish used in stocking, and between 1928 and 1933, the beginning of September weight of these fish was increased from an average of 2·1gm to 6·09gm, while the progeny of the individual matings were reaching 12·7gm. But whereas Embody and Heyford's fish had been extremely variable in growth rate, Lord and Davis found that the progeny of an individual mating all closely resembled one another; that is to say, the strain was beginning to breed true to type, and this end had been hastened by choosing the breeding stock for a new generation from fish of a good, even-sized group rather than from outstanding specimens of several variable groups. This is now common practice in pig breeding in this country, for the most useful sow or boar is one which produces litters of even and fast growth rather than one or two giants among a group of runts.

Quite apart from the steady improvement in growth rate, other improvements had been noted. The fast-growing fish were more prolific, and the number of ova per pound of body weight of Brook Trout had been increased by about 20 per cent, and at the same time there had been the steady increase in the resistance to furunculosis of fast-growers, which had originally been noticed by Embody and

Heyford. In fact a furunculosis-resistant strain was being deliberately developed.

A check of the Pittsford results was made at Leetown Hatchery in 1933. At 29·5 weeks of age, wild fish averaged 4·6gm; fish from parents of one generation of domestication averaged 4·9gm, and the fish hatched from Pittsford eggs averaged 11·5gm. These results are impressive in themselves, but become more so when we refer to the health of the stocks.

When the Leetown check commenced there were 1,200 fish in each group. An outbreak of furunculosis occurred and was allowed to proceed without attempt at control. Of the wild fish, no fewer than 718 died; of the fish from parents of one generation of domestication 546 died, but of the fish hatched from Pittsford eggs only 169 died.

The combination of fast-growth, increased prolificacy and heightened resistance prompts one to feel that it is not so much that a new characteristic was bred into the fish as that several undesirable characteristics were selected out.

It was always noticed that when eggs from a number of different sources were used in one hatchery, quite serious mortality occurred in all groups except that of local origin, and Dr Davis suggested in 1930 that the trout culturalist should raise his own selected strain of fish from the stock native to the hatchery district. It is doubtful whether the advice still holds good, for the use of eggs of an improved strain may save several years' work, and the fact that some fish survive in their new environment means that they have acclimatized themselves. The eggs from which the Ennis Hatchery, Montana, raised its fast-growing Rainbow Trout were 'special' eggs imported from Birdview Hatchery, Washington, and the results there have been excellent.

All of the later breeding experiments were accompanied by others designed to determine the value of a hatchery-raised fish to the river fisherman. Results showed that the well-nourished trout released as a legal sized fish was at no disadvantage by comparison with the wild trout in a stream. He rose freely, fought well and satisfied his appetite, though apparently he did not often use plankton foods. Under difficult conditions for fishing he appeared to be quite as shy as a wild fish. Experiments in 1933 and 1934 confirmed the tendency of Rainbow Trout to move downstream, and in the latter year it was noticed that the hatchery fish were exceedingly difficult to catch. In more recent stocking experiments it has often been found that wild trout are more easily caught than newly introduced stock. This is believed to be due to the fact that the less well nourished wild fish are more easily tempted to seize a lure.

The flesh colour of trouts has been the subject of a great deal of argument. W.C.Kendall as long ago as 1918 stated that the factor for red coloration was something borne in the fish. If a fish had a genetic capacity to produce red flesh and were well nourished, his flesh would be red; on a low plane of nutrition his flesh would be pale, but no amount or quality of food would change to redness the flesh of a trout which had not the necessary genetic constitution. In recent years Holloway and Chamberlain found that hatchery fish soon recovered their redness when released in a stream or when held in a dirt-bottomed rearing pond. Their finding would seem to support the oft expressed conviction that some item of natural diet is responsible for redness, but of course it does not mean that Kendall is wrong, for there are many streams containing very pale fleshed trout. It would be interesting to find out if these became red when placed in a better feeding environment.

The Practical Importance of the American Experimental Work

The more quickly a trout can be brought to saleable size the lower per pound of fish produced are the costs of production. In Britain at this moment the vast majority of 8 to 9in fish used in stocking are 2-year-olds: fish which at 3 to 5in length were held through one winter eating $2\frac{1}{2}$ per cent of their body weight in food each day without making any growth. Fish which are stocked in their second spring will of course have been held through two winters.

All foods fed to growing trout are very high in protein, much higher than the food fed to farm livestock, and furthermore the food must contain a large percentage of fresh meat if the growth of the organs is to be normal.

No trout farmer can afford to feed fish without their making growth, for he relies for his income upon the amount of weight increase of his fish, and the longer fish are kept without putting on weight the more he is reducing his profit.

Selective breeding for high growth factor should make it easy to produce 8in fish by the end of the first summer, and the quantity of food used to produce 1lb of trout suitable for stocking would be reduced by reason of the fact that fast-growing fish are better food converters than slow-growers, and the fact that the fish were not fed over the winter period.

Dr M.E.Brown, working in Britain in 1946, found that it took 6lb of meat to produce 1lb of trout. This is much less than the figure given me by a well-known fish farmer of 10lb of food to produce 1lb of trout, but of course his 10lb of food may be much cheaper than the 6lb of meat. Both these figures are much too high and compare very badly with the conversion figures of the Ennis Hatchery.

115

Ennis is a 'production' hatchery, not an experimental establishment, and it operates as a unit of the US Fish and Wildlife Service. During 1950 they raised 32,574lb of trout by feeding to them 85,360lb of horse flesh, 1,742lb of horse liver, 19,069lb of beef tripe, and 838lb of brewer's yeast. This represents 1lb of trout from every 3·77lb of food. These figures were given to me by Dr Meehean and Mr Hagen of the Fish and Wildlife Service and are unquestionably correct. They are considered too high by the hatchery management, and although the 1951 figures are not yet available it is known that they show a better food conversion ratio than the 1950 figures. In some of the experimental work in the 1930's it was often found possible to produce 1lb of fish for as little as 2lb of highly concentrated foods.

In 1945 it cost 22¢ to raise 1lb of trout on a meat diet but the use of 50 per cent of high protein meal reduced the cost of the food to 12¢ per 1b of trout flesh. At this moment we in Britain are paying 7s 6d to 14s per 1b for the trout used in stocking (1,000 × 8in fish at 2 years of age cost approximately £75 and their weight is 200lb; 1,000 × 5in yearlings cost £35 and weigh only 50lb). Even when we take into consideration the heavy labour costs and overheads of commercial trout production we must still conclude that our fish are costing too much.

The use of fast-growing fish would enable hatcheries to use their foods more economically, and because trout were released after a shorter period in the rearing pools and raceways, increased output would lower the overheads. I have been told that it would be pointless to increase output because the existing demand does not justify it. What rubbish this is! The existing demand is low because prices are too high. Very few associations can afford to stock their waters adequately at the moment, but if the price were reduced to £40 to £50 per thousand for 8in fish many associations would increase their stocking commitments, and many others would swing from coarse fish to trout. We should not forget that Continental Rainbow Trout are sold as food in Britain for as little as 3s 3d per 1b retail, and that 4s to 5s per 1b for home produced stock fish should therefore be an adequate price. It is true that at least some of the imported Rainbows are produced in sewage ponds, but they are no less valuable for all that, and if they can be produced cheaply by such means it is up to us to learn how to do it: not condemn the Germans and Dutch for their enterprise.

Whether or not the Continental farmers have improved their strains of Rainbow Trout I do not know, but certainly the Americans have achieved results which are little short of miraculous.

I have examined a number of documents originating in both this country and USA in order to get a clear picture of the classification of the Rainbow. The only account which was fully satisfying was that written by Dr E.B.Worthington published in *The Salmon and Trout Magazine* (Nos100 and 101).

The Americans seem to have done with their Rainbow classification exactly the same thing that we did with our Brown Trout, that is to say they have given races the status of species. In addition, several scientists have revised the classification so that several names exist for the one race of fish.

Much of the classification relied upon differences in the scale counts of the lateral line, but later it was shown that this method was invalid because the variation appeared when fish of the same stock were reared in waters of differing temperature. Quite recently it was reported in *Fishing Gazette* that American workers had found it possible to increase the number of vertebrae by subjecting the ova to shock treatment by quick freezing. Such shocks occur naturally from time to time, and result in specimens which are slightly different from the original stock; nevertheless they are of the same species since these differences are environmental rather than genetical.

The most useful classification of the Rainbow Trout is that which ignores the appearance of the types and relies upon their differences of habit. The method was adopted by Worthington and has the advantage that it is of practical importance.

The name *Salmo gairdnerii* is given to the migratory Rainbow Trout known as the Steelhead and which corresponds to our Sea Trout. (The word Steelhead has also been used in the USA to describe the migratory type of Dolly Varden Trout, *Salvelinus Malma*.) *Salmo irideus* is the Rainbow Trout of the Pacific coastal rivers. It is partly migratory and a spring spawner and is the predominant type used in stocking work in Britain. *Salmo shasta* is the fast-growing, non-migratory, November spawning fish which originated in the McCloud River near Mt Shasta, California. Although not given by Worthington as a separate type, the Kamloops Trout, a Rainbow native to Lake Kamloops, has such amazingly fast growth that it deserves mention. In Lake Pend Oreille, Washington, these fish have reached 40lb in weight by the end of their fourth summer. The water teems with a degenerate race of land-locked salmon and this fact no doubt has greatly contributed to the rapidity of growth. Haig-Brown refers to the Kamloops Rainbow in his book *A River Never Sleeps* and states that these fish spawn at the end of their fourth year. Other races of Rainbow Trout spawn at three or even two years of age and the Kamloops Trout thus appears to enjoy a longer period of uninterrupted weight increase and incidentally avoids for an extra twelve months the complications of spawning to which I refer below.

The Ennis Hatchery has used Rainbow Trout for its selective

breeding work, and today 80 per cent of their yearling output consists of 9in fish while the remaining 20 per cent of yearlings weigh over 1lb. The hatchery enjoys an exceptionally useful supply of water which remains at or near 54°F all the year round; growth is thus continuous through the twelve months. Nonetheless eggs from wild-bred parents will not give such good results.

The strain of fast-growing fish was developed at Ennis to enable the hatchery to stock the streams of the area with 3 to 7in long fish in early summer. Stocking in autumn gave poor recovery rates but the summer stocked fish grew away well, and were able to acclimatize themselves to withstand the winter conditions of the water. Any tendency for the trout to spawn in spring had to be selected out and all the brood fish are now winter spawners. The fry are frequently graded during rearing to ensure that large specimens selected for breeding are not merely the result of social hierarchy resulting from a slightly stronger fish getting more food than his fellows and being thus able to increase his lead over the others. The Ennis fish are made to compete against others of their own size.

Perhaps the greatest drawback of our Rainbow stocks is their tendency to spawn in spring. In one of the published articles on Rainbows that came my way, an English trout farmer stated that he had found it convenient to use spring-spawning fish as brood stock, so that he could hatch his Rainbows after the Brown Trout hatch. Again, another breeder admitted to me in conversation that he used spring spawning fish in order to make up the number of Rainbow eggs. Clearly, both these workers have perpetuated the nuisance we seek to avoid; spring-spawners should not be used as brood stock if the progeny are to be placed in a water containing Brown Trout: on their own, it would be possible to open and close the season later.

Much has been written of the disappearance of Rainbow Trout. Some of the reasons given have been so ludicrous as to savour of magical intervention. The fact is that Rainbow Trout are shorter lived than Brown Trout and at the same time the existing stocks contain a lot of migratory blood and some fish will leave the water by any exit available. Shasta Rainbows were imported by Mr D.F. Leney in 1932 and others have come in since, but there is little doubt that all *Shasta* stocks, no matter what their origin, have the *Irideus* taint, for the United States workers had been moving fish from river to river for many years before it was realized that there were important differences of habit between the races. Hildebrand expressly refers to this matter in his paper. The fact that mixing has taken place does not mean that the required qualities have been lost for ever. Mendelian law shows that a characteristic is lost only when the carrier is prevented from breeding. It would be readily possible to regain a race of non-migratory fish by permitting migration and using for brood stock those fish which did not migrate, in other words the migratory tendency would be selected out naturally, provided fish which migrated were unable to return.

It is possible that this has already occurred in Lough Shure, Arranmore, the only acid water in Britain in which Rainbows have been known to breed. These fish were stocked in 1905, and undoubtedly those which had the urge to travel would have left the lake by the 300ft fall at the exit. The present stock of fish should form an interesting breeding nucleus for stocking other acid waters; it would also be interesting to find out whether they retained their non-migratory tendency when transplanted.

The tendency for Rainbow Trout to be short lived has often been associated with unsatisfactory spawning conditions under which many trout become egg bound. Both Leach and Worthington offer evidence of the necessity of running water, gravel bottom and an attendant male fish if the female is to spawn successfully. There is little doubt that careful preparation of feeder streams would lower mortality due to egg-bound condition. That the hen fish live to a ripe old age when stripped in a hatchery every year is borne out by Mr D.F. Leney's experience of two Rainbows hatched from his imported *Shasta* eggs. The fish reached 10lb in weight in their eighth year and were each stripped four or five times.

The Rainbow Trout has such excellent qualities that its use should be encouraged by the necessary breeding work to eliminate the undesirable factors which are undoubtedly present. The species is able to thrive in water of a slightly lower oxygen content than that suitable for Brown Trout, and for this reason is better able to withstand pollution and high water temperatures: in hot weather when Brown Trout are deep down and dour the Rainbow will rise freely and fight like a demon. In addition to its better sporting qualities we must add that its flesh is deeply coloured and of excellent flavour. Both of its disadvantages can be overcome by selective breeding.

Undoubtedly the best method would be to stock them on their own and manage the water as a Rainbow fishery. An association having two lakes could stock spring spawning Rainbows in the one and Brown Trout in the other, and thereby enjoy a nine month trout season. If on the other hand an autumn spawning strain of Rainbows were available, a Brown Trout water would provide better sport in summer time if the stock included 10 or 15 per cent of Rainbows, allowance being made for their faster growth by reducing the total number of fish stocked by 15 per cent. Although I have no concrete example of its efficacy, it may well be that biological control of a vermin population could be achieved by stocking Rainbow Trout in place of Brown Trout. I have little doubt that the larger appetite and greater vigour of Rainbows would enable them to compete against a coarse species and reduce the fry population far better than can the Brown Trout.

Perhaps, reader, you have gathered an impression that only the Rainbow stocks of this country need to be improved; this is far from being the case: the Brown Trout is also a very variable quantity. I have occasionally noticed a condition of egg binding in females, and earlier in this book I mentioned the tendency of many of the fish to spawn after the season had opened. We must face the fact that our stocks of fish are well below standard, either as a result of chance methods of breeding or because the type used has been selected for the convenience of the hatchery manager rather than for its suitability as a sporting fish. So far as lake management is concerned spawning streams would be a great help. There is no reason why spawning should interfere with stocking, if, after spawning, the water is diverted down another channel to cause the death of the eggs.

From time to time the policy of in-breeding becomes the subject of most unfair criticism. It is quite true, of course, that the mating of close relatives does produce physical and mental freaks, but it does so only because the parent stock had these weaknesses to a lesser degree. The trouble appears to occur when breeders try to improve the beauty of an animal rather than its utility. Beauty lies in the eye of the beholder, and judging by the appearance of some of our modern show gun dogs there can be many conceptions of beauty and few have much bearing on field work. If arbitrarily members of a breed society decide to develop an animal with a longer head and narrower skull, automatically they will have to mate specimens which are not typical, and in the quest for the 'new look' fine boned animals with poor stamina are quite likely to be used and the result of their mating may well be undesirable specimens. In-breeding can only be successful when the parent stock is sound.

Line-breeding was blamed for the barrenness which developed in the brood stock held at the hatchery of the Pemberton-Warren Trout Acclimatization Society of Western Australia. Some of the fish stripped in recent years were 4-year-olds and it is possible that some of them had become barren as a result of faulty stripping in the previous year with consequent rupture of the ovarian membrane; this possibility will not, however, account for more than a very small percentage of the barrenness.

In the society's report for 1948, mention is made of the fact that many 3-year-olds had no spawn. In the following year these fish appear to have been spawned as 4-year-olds and a factor for late maturity rather than barrenness would thus have been perpetuated.

Lack of colour of the brood stock was also noticed and because of the deficiencies of the domesticated stock it was decided to use 'wild' fish for future stripping. Whether or not this policy will prove a satisfactory one I cannot say, for the fish trapped from the streams were originally bred in the hatchery and must carry the same undesirable factors as the domesticated fish.[1]

Selection of brood stock was on a basis of fast-growth and early season maturity; prolificacy, body conformation, good coloration and youthful maturity are not mentioned as having formed part of the basis of the selection and one can only presume that their omission resulted in a greater part of the society's breeding misfortunes.

In all the breeding work, mass selection methods were used rather than individual matings. These methods must always be dangerous because one does not eliminate undersirable fish. Complete control of in-breeding work is essential.

The Future Development of our Fisheries

It is all too easy to blame those who have bred our existing stocks for their present lack of quality. But before we do so let us examine the difficulties under which the fish-farmer works in Britain.

Meat, offal and high protein meals are in very short supply, and the farmer has great difficulty in obtaining enough high quality foods to feed commercial stocks let alone experimental groups. The British trout farmer paddles his own canoe: he has to pay for his own experience, there is no adequate organization to carry out research on his behalf and solve his many problems for him. Although there is a Brown Trout Research Station at Pitlochry, its work has so far been of academic interest rather than practical importance. In many ways the research is parallel to that of FBA at Windermere, although it is clear that large scale experiments with artificial fertilizers will shortly be undertaken in an attempt to increase the crops of trout. Nothing of the work accomplished so far has any value to the trout farmer, and it would appear that the scientists are happy to work with our existing unimproved stocks of fish. Surely, work to improve the quality of the fish should be proceeding side by side with work to increase the fertility and resultant productivity of the water!

The most encouraging news in the reports of the station's work is

1. Since writing the above, I have had a letter from Mr A. R. Kelly, the manager of the Pemberton Hatchery, and he confirms that since the Association reverted to the stripping of wild fish, the stocks have shown much earlier maturity. At the same time important changes in the diet of the fish were made and both Crayfish meal and Di-caltic Phosphate are being used. It is thus, he says, quite impossible to attribute the improvement solely to a changed breeding policy.

I feel it is most unfortunate that a small group of fish was not held on the old diet, so that it was possible to observe the influence of the new diet.

that Derris extract was used in Loch Kinardochy in 1949 and again in 1950 to exterminate the pike population. The use of the substance in experimental work does not however mean that its use would be generally sanctioned.

By contrast the Fish and Wildlife Service and the State Governments in USA are operating many experimental hatcheries staffed with research workers and the information so gained is passed on to the industry. In 1949, research staff engaged upon the problems of freshwater fishery management totalled 324 and the expenditure on research work was $1,473,448.

At one time it was easy for the small business to work out its own salvation. Particularly was this true when materials and labour were cheap, for one could then afford to use both on enterprises from which there was no direct profit. Experimental work today is a matter of costs, and hit or miss methods are too expensive. This in turn means that the research work has to be undertaken by a trained – and sometimes highly paid – scientist, and only the highly capitalized companies can afford to run their own research departments. Some industries have pooled their resources to set up a joint research centre to solve problems for the industry as a whole, and in other cases the responsibility for the research is undertaken by a government department. An example of this last type of research and advisory organization is the National Agricultural Advisory Service which exists to serve every farmer in the country . . . except the fish farmer.

It is true that the FBA can help with water problems, but primarily the organization exists for pure research, not for applied fishery research and experimental work in hatchery techniques. The Ministry of Agriculture and Fisheries has taken little interest in freshwater matters and when recent legislation threatened to undermine the ability of riparian owners to protect the water from pollution, it was not the Ministry but the fishermen who through ACA, their pollution fighting organization, strove successfully to ensure that the Common Law right of the riparian owner was retained in the bill to act as a check upon the actions of the new River Boards whose members are predominantly dwellers in industrial towns.

Reluctantly, I have come to the conclusion that our inland fisheries have suffered neglect by reason of the fact that they fall under the jurisdiction of the Fisheries Department of the Ministry of Agriculture. This department with its laboratory and library in Lowestoft has always shown itself interested chiefly in our sea fishing industry. There is little doubt that inland fisheries would be much better off were they legislated for and administered by the agricultural section of the Ministry, when fishery work would become another department of NAAS and the agricultural research centres.

Every angler should be aware of the fact, that in America inland waters are used jointly for food production and sport, and under the Farm Fish Ponds Scheme some 270,000 ponds have been made in the last ten years or so. In many cases the farmer has been given a subsidy on the constructional work, and his stock fish are always supplied free of charge. Land so used is producing more flesh per acre than it would by grazing – even were the pastures as good as ours.

Our inland fisheries are a disgrace to any progressive society. It is not enough for ACA and similar organizations to fight the polluter: we need a positive approach to the whole matter of the usage of our waters. What is the gain if we stop them being used for unlawful purposes, and do not then ensure that they are made to be productive of useful game fish to provide food and sport.

Our angling associations must share the blame. All too seldom do they attempt to interest their members in conservation: a great majority of the societies exist merely as a means of raising money to rent a fishery and there is no attempt to manage the water and make it productive. In the industrial North the pollution of the rivers and diminution of the size of the average fish has made contest fishing the only sport possible in many areas; the anglers are satisfied to catch tiddlers provided they catch enough of them. Surely as a gifted nation we can achieve something better than this as an angling recreation!

So far as game fishes are concerned, improvement of stock will have to be on a nationwide basis. Good brood stock may exist anywhere and it is very probable that there are better naturally bred fish in some of our waters than exist in the hatcheries. When really fine specimens are caught in a water containing marked fish, they should not be killed, but should be transferred to a holding pond for possible use as breeders. It would be simple enough to check their value for that purpose against the stock already held in the hatchery.

CHAPTER FOURTEEN

....

Books About Fish and Fishing

BELOW IS A SHORT LIST of the books which I have found most helpful in forming my angling technique and in writing this book:

GAME SPECIES

1) A Trout and Salmon Fisherman for Seventy Five Years, by E.R.Hewitt. Scribner; New York
2) Salmon Fishing: A New Philosophy, by R.Waddington. Peter Davies
3) The Life of the Sea Trout, by G.H.Nall. Seeley, Service
4) The Practical Angler, by W.C.Stewart. Black
5) The Way of a Trout with a Fly, by G.E.M.Skues. Black
6) Wye Salmon and Other Fish, by J.A.Hutton. Sherratt

TACKLE

7) La Canne à Mouche à Truite, Objet d'Art, by Joannès Robin. Bosc Frères, Lyon
8) Professional Fly Tying and Tackle Making, by G.L.Herter. Herter; Waseca, Minnesota
9) Professional Split Bamboo Rod Building Manual, by G.L.Herter. Herter; Waseca, Minnesota
10) Rod Building for Amateurs, by Richard Walker. Belfield & Bushell

Robin's is undoubtedly the best book ever written on fly rods. I do not think that there is an English translation available, but the book is quite easy to read in the original.

Robin's method of assessing the value of a rod is based upon analysis of its curve under a given load. He states, and I agree with his statement, that a multiplicity of rod actions is unnecessary: there must be one action more efficient than all others and that same action could be had in different lengths and weights. A method which would enable a maker to price his rods according to their performance rather than their appearance should not lightly be set aside. Of the rods he examined, a 'Halford Knockabout' by Messrs Hardy Bros showed as good a performance as any.

Mr Herter's two books are probably the most complete on these subjects available. The writer is a manufacturer of some importance in America.

Rod Building for Amateurs is a shorter book than either of Mr Herter's but is nevertheless very complete. Mr Walker is an engineer, a wonderful craftsman and above all a superlatively good fisherman well able to check the value of his ideas before putting them on paper.

FRESHWATER BIOLOGY

11) Blue Green Algae, by G.E.Fogg. New Biology No5, Penguin
12) Control of Algae, by F.E.Hale. US Waterworks & Sewerage Magazine, 1939
13) Copper Sulphate, by Paul Weir. US Waterworks & Sewerage Magazine, June 1945
14) Effect of Copper Sulphate on Organisms, by Paul Weir. US Waterworks & Sewerage Magazine, May 1939
15) Freshwater Biology and Water Supply in Britain, by W.H.Pearsall, A.C.Gardiner and F.Greenshield. The Freshwater Biological Association, Windermere
16) Freshwater Life of the British Isles, by John Clegg. Warne
17) Freshwater Snails, by T.T.Macan. Country Sportsman, February 1949
18) Life in Inland Waters, by Kathleen Carpenter. Sidgwick & Jackson
19) Life in Lakes and Rivers, by T.T.Macan and E.B.Worthington. Collins
20) Industrial Wastes and Fish Life, by M.Ellis. US Waterworks & Sewerage Magazine, May 1945
21) Progress in Biological Enquiries, published yearly from 1928 to 1939. US Fish and Wildlife Service, Washington
22) The English Lakes and Their Development, by W.H.Pearsall. New Biology No6, Penguin
23) The Freshwater Shrimp, by T.T.Macan. Country Sportsman, March 1950
24) The Reaction and Resistance of Fishes in their Natural Environment to Acidity, Alkalinity and Neutrality, by M.W.Wells. US Biological Bulletin, October 1915
25) Water Supply Today, by John Bowman. Oxford University Press

Pure research in connection with freshwater is as far advanced in England as it is anywhere in the world, but it is true to say that it is easier to obtain information from United States sources than from our own. As yet we have not compiled complete bibliographies in the way that the American Information Service has, and much of the valuable work carried out and published by our scientists remains hidden away in little known journals which are filed by the researcher but which are completely unknown to the man who could make practical use of the information.

No15 on the above list is a brief but complete account of water, algae, plankton crops, algicides, stratification and water sampling.

No19, *Life in Lakes and Rivers*, is a book which should be in every fisherman's possession. It is well written, beautifully illustrated and has the great advantage that the authors explain their terms as they go along.

The Reports of Progress in Biological Enquiries contain not only accounts of the work on Wisconsin lakes by Professors Birge and Juday but also accounts of the experiments on Trout Breeding, Disease Resistance and so on which were carried out at Pittsford, Vermont; Hackettstown, New Jersey; Leetown and elsewhere.

Water Supply Today is written from the water engineer's viewpoint: a viewpoint which should be appreciated by those who fish in reservoirs.

FISH AND FISH CULTURE

26) Artificial Propagation of Brook Trout and Rainbow Trout with Notes on three other Species, by G.C.Leach. US Fisheries Document No955
27) Care and Diseases of Trout, by H.S.Davis. US Research Report No12, 1947
28) Commercial Trout Culture, Fisheries Notice No29, Ministry of Agriculture and Fisheries, 1950
29) Disease Control in Hatchery Fish, by F.F.Fish. US Fishery Leaflet No68
30) Fishes, Their Way of Life, by Louis Roule. Routledge
31) Peculiarities of Rainbow Trout, by S.A.Young. Salmon and Trout Magazine No100, September 1939
32) Rainbows in Acid Water, by Winifred Frost. Salmon and Trout Magazine No100, September 1939
33) Sewage Disposal in Germany, by Dr Ing. Karl Imhoff. US Waterworks and Sewerage Magazine, March 1939
34) Some Publications on Diseases and Parasites of Fishes, US Fishery Leaflet No58, 1947
35) Some Publications on Fish Culture and Related Subjects, US Fishery Leaflet No6, 1950
36) Survey of Fish Culture in the United States, by A.V.Tunison, C.Mullin and O.L.Meehean, 1949
37) The Culture of Fish in Ponds, by C.B.Hall. Ministry of Agriculture & Fisheries Bulletin No12, 1930
38) The Effect of Slightly Alkaline Tap Water upon Spawn and Eggs of Trout and Perch, by E.S.Hopkins. Journal of American Water Works Association, 1928
39) The Food of Coarse Fish by P.H.T.Hartley. Freshwater Biological Association, Windermere
40) The Nutrition of Fish in Hatcheries; a Literature Survey by N.Karrick. US Fishery Leaflet No325, 1948
41) The Pemberton-Warren (Western Australia) Trout Acclimatization Society's Annual Reports Nos17 (1948), 18 (1949), 19 (1950) and 20 (1951)
42) The Production of Freshwater Fish for Food by T.T.Macan, C.H. Mortimer and E.B.Worthington. Scientific Publication No6 of the Freshwater Biological Association at Windermere
43) The Second and Third Annual Reports of the Supervisory Committee for Brown Trout Research. HMSO Edinburgh, 1951 and 1952
44) The Story of the Fish, by Brian Curtis. Jonathan Cape
45) The Trouts of North America, by S.F.Hildebrand. US Fishery Leaflet No355, 1949
46) Trout Feeds and Feeding, by A.V.Tunison. US Fish and Wildlife Service, 1945

In his book *The Story of the Fish* Mr Curtis made it his object to collect from little known scientific papers facts of interest to fishermen. He has succeeded in presenting interesting matter in an easily read form.

The reports of the Pemberton-Warren Association are an example of thoroughness worthy of copy by all angling associations. The members are made familiar with the technical side of fishery management. The way in which this association has overcome its difficulties is an exciting romance in itself.

Mr Tunison's paper on Trout Feeding (No46) gives very full information on every aspect of the subject, from the mechanical preparation of the foodstuffs to the relationship between the quantities fed and the length of the fish and the water temperature.

FISHERY MANAGEMENT

47) Aquatic Plant Control with 2, 4-D, by S.W.Surber. US Fishery Leaflet No344, 1949
48) Available Publications on Fisheries. US Fishery Leaflet No9, 1951
49) Construction of Farm Fish Ponds, by J.M.Lawrence. Alabama Polytechnic Institute
50) Construction of Farm Ponds. US Fishery Leaflet No17, 1951
51) Farm Fish Ponds and Their Management, by O.L.Meehean. US Fishery Leaflet No27, 1945.
52) Farm Ponds, by M.T.Gowder & D.P.Schwab. Publication No333 of the Agricultural Extension Service, University of Tennessee
53) Fertilization of Ponds, by Krügel & Heinrich. International Illustrated Fertilizer Review, June 1939
54) Fish Stocking, by Meehean, James & Douglass. US Conservation Bulletin No35, 1944
55) Management of Farm Fish Ponds, by H.S.Swingle and E.V.Smith, Alabama Polytechnic Institute
56) Rainbows, a Report on Attempts to Acclimatize Rainbow Trout in Britain, by E.B.Worthington. Salmon & Trout Magazine, September 1939 and January 1940
57) Summary of Trout Stocking Experiments, by A.D.Holloway. US Fishery Leaflet No137, 1945
58) The Control of Aquatic Plants in Ponds and Lakes, by E.W.Surber. US Fishery Leaflet No217, 1948
59) The Use of Rotenone as a Fish Poison. US Fishery Leaflet No350
60) Vital Statistics of Fish Populations, by G.L.Kesteven. New Biology No4, Penguin
61) Weed Control in Small Ponds, by H.W.Jackson. Virginia Polytechnic Institute

Of the papers on pond construction No49 is the most complete from the technical point of view. No55 on pond management is excellently illustrated and clearly demonstrates how fine is the dividing line between success and failure when stocking with a food species.

Dr Worthington's report and conclusions are extremely important; no stocking-committee can afford to be ignorant of them.

MISCELLANEOUS BOOKS

62) A Dictionary of Biology, by M.Abercrombie, C.J.Hickman and M.L. Johnson. Penguin
63) Animal Breeding, by A.L.Hagedoorn. Crosby Lockwood
64) Genetics, by Hans Kalmus. Penguin

No62 is a most helpful book and one which I use frequently. It will enable the average angler to learn the terminology of the scientist. The ordinary English dictionary seldom gives satisfying meanings of scientific terms and a specialized dictionary of this type is essential.

No64 gives a clear explanation of inheritance, while No63 is a book with which every breeder of animals (and the word includes 'fish') should be familiar. There cannot be improvement in our fish stocks until breeders follow genetically sound principles.

HOW TO OBTAIN SCIENTIFIC AND OTHER PUBLICATIONS

Most books are quite easily obtained through the National Library Service, but scientific papers have a very limited distribution and in some cases there may be but two or three copies in the whole country. The local librarian cannot be expected easily to obtain such publications even if they are available for loan. It is often necessary for the would be borrower to tell the librarian where copies of the publication are kept.

Because I had much difficulty in obtaining many of the papers and articles used in compiling this book, I have made the following notes which may be of assistance to others:

Nos8 and 9 were imported direct on a Board of Trade Import Licence. No8 costs $1.50 and No9 $1.25.

Nos12, 13, 14, 20, 24, 33 and 38 may be obtained from the Library of the Science Museum through the Library Service.

Nos21, 26, 27, 29, 34, 35, 36, 40, 45, 46, 47, 48, 50, 51, 54, 57, 58 and 59 may be obtained direct from the office of the United States Federal Fish & Wildlife Service, at the Department of the Interior, Washington, D.C., free of charge. Some of the reports of 'Progress in Biological Enquiries' are no longer obtainable. Many of these United States publications are held by the Librarian of the Fisheries Laboratory, Ministry of Agriculture & Fisheries, Lowestoft, and this library holds copies of all the reports, 'Progress in Biological Enquiries' referred to in this book.

Nos49, 52, 55 and 61 may be obtained free of charge from the librarians of the publishing colleges. I would like to mention that I have never been refused literature by any of the American authorities to whom I have written.

Nos31, 32 and 56 are still obtainable from the Salmon & Trout Association, at Fishmongers' Hall; alternatively they may be borrowed from the Librarian of the Fisheries' Laboratory, Lowestoft, through the Library Service.

No53 is available in the Library of Rothamsted Agricultural Research Station.

It is unfortunate that some libraries, such as that of the Freshwater Biological Association, do not permit books to leave the premises. Relatively few people are able to afford to journey perhaps several hundred miles to refer to a book and it is a pity that it is not possible to have books transferred to the reference room of the local library where they could be consulted under proper supervision.